ISO IEC 27002
Complete Self-Assessment Gui

C000099268

The guidance in this Self-Assessment i:
practices and standards in business process arcn~~itecture, desig~~n and
quality management. The guidance is also based on the professional
judgment of the individual collaborators listed in the Acknowledgments.

Notice of rights

Table of Contents

About The Art of Service

The Art of Service, Business Process Architects since 2000, is dedicated to helping stakeholders achieve excellence.

Defining, designing, creating, and implementing a process to solve a stakeholders challenge or meet an objective is the most valuable role… In EVERY group, company, organization and department.

Unless you're talking a one-time, single-use project, there should be a process. Whether that process is managed and implemented by humans, AI, or a combination of the two, it needs to be designed by someone with a complex enough perspective to ask the right questions.

Someone capable of asking the right questions and step back and say, 'What are we really trying to accomplish here? And is there a different way to look at it?'

With The Art of Service's Standard Requirements Self-Assessments, we empower people who can do just that — whether their title is marketer, entrepreneur, manager, salesperson, consultant, Business Process Manager, executive assistant, IT Manager, CIO etc... —they are the people who rule the future. They are people who watch the process as it happens, and ask the right questions to make the process work better.

Contact us when you need any support with this Self-Assessment and any help with templates, blue-prints and examples of standard documents you might need:

http://theartofservice.com
service@theartofservice.com

Included Resources - how to access

Included with your purchase of the book is the ISO IEC 27002

Self-Assessment Spreadsheet Dashboard which contains all questions and Self-Assessment areas and auto-generates insights, graphs, and project RACI planning - all with examples to get you started right away.

How? Simply send an email to
access@theartofservice.com
with this books' title in the subject to get the ISO IEC 27002 Self Assessment Tool right away.

You will receive the following contents with New and Updated specific criteria:

- The latest quick edition of the book in PDF

- The latest complete edition of the book in PDF, which criteria correspond to the criteria in...

- The Self-Assessment Excel Dashboard, and...

- Example pre-filled Self-Assessment Excel Dashboard to get familiar with results generation

- In-depth specific Checklists covering the topic

- Project management checklists and templates to assist with implementation

INCLUDES LIFETIME SELF ASSESSMENT UPDATES

Every self assessment comes with Lifetime Updates and Lifetime Free Updated Books. Lifetime Updates is an industry-first feature which allows you to receive verified self assessment updates, ensuring you always have the most accurate information at your fingertips.

Get it now- you will be glad you did - do it now, before you forget.

Send an email to **access@theartofservice.com** with this books' title in the subject to get the ISO IEC 27002 Self Assessment Tool right away.

Purpose of this Self-Assessment

This Self-Assessment has been developed to improve understanding of the requirements and elements of ISO IEC 27002, based on best practices and standards in business process architecture, design and quality management.

It is designed to allow for a rapid Self-Assessment to determine how closely existing management practices and procedures correspond to the elements of the Self-Assessment.

The criteria of requirements and elements of ISO IEC 27002 have been rephrased in the format of a Self-Assessment questionnaire, with a seven-criterion scoring system, as explained in this document.

In this format, even with limited background knowledge of ISO IEC 27002, a manager can quickly review existing operations to determine how they measure up to the standards. This in turn can serve as the starting point of a 'gap analysis' to identify management tools or system elements that might usefully be implemented in the organization to help improve overall performance.

How to use the Self-Assessment

On the following pages are a series of questions to identify to what extent your ISO IEC 27002 initiative is complete in comparison to the requirements set in standards.

To facilitate answering the questions, there is a space in front of each question to enter a score on a scale of '1' to '5'.

1 Strongly Disagree

2 Disagree

3 Neutral

4 Agree

5 Strongly Agree

Read the question and rate it with the following in front of mind:

'In my belief, the answer to this question is clearly defined'.

There are two ways in which you can choose to interpret this statement;
1. how aware are you that the answer to the question is clearly defined
2. for more in-depth analysis you can choose to gather evidence and confirm the answer to the question. This obviously will take more time, most Self-Assessment users opt for the first way to interpret the question and dig deeper later on based on the outcome of the overall Self-Assessment.

A score of '1' would mean that the answer is not clear at all, where a '5' would mean the answer is crystal clear and defined. Leave emtpy when the question is not applicable or you don't want to answer it, you can skip it without affecting your score. Write your score in the space provided.

After you have responded to all the appropriate statements in each section, compute your average score for that section, using the formula provided, and round to the nearest tenth. Then transfer to the corresponding spoke in the ISO IEC 27002 Scorecard on the second next page of the Self-Assessment.

Your completed ISO IEC 27002 Scorecard will give you a clear presentation of which ISO IEC 27002 areas need attention.

ISO IEC 27002
Scorecard Example

Example of how the finalized Scorecard can look like:

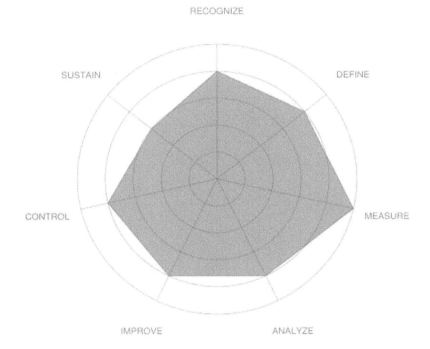

ISO IEC 27002
Scorecard

Your Scores:

BEGINNING OF THE SELF-ASSESSMENT:

CRITERION #1: RECOGNIZE

INTENT: Be aware of the need for change. Recognize that there is an unfavorable variation, problem or symptom.

In my belief, the answer to this question is clearly defined:

5 Strongly Agree

4 Agree

3 Neutral

2 Disagree

1 Strongly Disagree

1. Are employees recognized or rewarded for performance that demonstrates the highest levels of integrity?
<--- Score

2. What does ISO IEC 27002 success mean to the stakeholders?
<--- Score

3. Do you need different information or graphics?
<--- Score

4. What are the stakeholder objectives to be achieved with ISO IEC 27002?
<--- Score

5. Do you need to address or achieve all of the control objectives in ISO/IEC 27002?
<--- Score

6. How do you identify the kinds of information that you will need?
<--- Score

7. Do you make sure that your organizations contractors receive the information security training and education others need to do jobs?
<--- Score

8. Do you identify responsibilities still valid after termination of employment?
<--- Score

9. What needs to be done?
<--- Score

10. Do you ask suppliers to identify critical product and service components?
<--- Score

11. Personally identifiable information protection?
<--- Score

12. Who clarifies your resilience and recovery needs and requirements?

<--- Score

13. Are there any revenue recognition issues?
<--- Score

14. Do you protect all relevant personally identifiable information?
<--- Score

15. What would happen if ISO IEC 27002 weren't done?
<--- Score

16. Do you create notification procedures to address screening issues?
<--- Score

17. Do you ask suppiers to identify critical product and service components?
<--- Score

18. Do you follow up on compliance and performance problems?
<--- Score

19. Do you identify old responsibilities still valid after job duties change?
<--- Score

20. Do you ask suppliers to notify you if others uncover security issues?
<--- Score

21. Did you identify the types of suppliers that will be allowed to have access?
<--- Score

22. What techniques can identify incidents?
<--- Score

23. What else needs to be measured?
<--- Score

24. What situation(s) led to this ISO IEC 27002 Self Assessment?
<--- Score

25. Are problem definition and motivation clearly presented?
<--- Score

26. Who needs what information?
<--- Score

27. What are the timeframes required to resolve each of the issues/problems?
<--- Score

28. What are your needs in relation to ISO IEC 27002 skills, labor, equipment, and markets?
<--- Score

29. What are the minority interests and what amount of minority interests can be recognized?
<--- Score

30. Do you make sure that employees receive the information security training and education others need to properly carry out jobs?
<--- Score

31. What problems are you facing and how do

you consider ISO IEC 27002 will circumvent those obstacles?
<--- Score

32. As a sponsor, customer or management, how important is it to meet goals, objectives?
<--- Score

33. Do you identify contacts for each information security agreement?
<--- Score

34. Which information does the ISO IEC 27002 business case need to include?
<--- Score

35. Do you review operational problems, failures, faults, and disruptions?
<--- Score

36. Do you ask suppliers to notify you if they uncover security issues?
<--- Score

37. Do you identify newly acquired information security responsibilities?
<--- Score

38. Do you ask suppliers to share information about potential problems?
<--- Score

39. Do you resolve identified problems, failures, faults, and disruptions?
<--- Score

40. Do you ask suppliers to account for how security issues were resolved?
<--- Score

41. What are the specific security management issues for telecommunications organizations?
<--- Score

42. How are the ISO IEC 27002's objectives aligned to the group's overall stakeholder strategy?
<--- Score

43. Are there any specific expectations or concerns about the ISO IEC 27002 team, ISO IEC 27002 itself?
<--- Score

44. Do you review supplier audit trails and records of security events?
<--- Score

45. What are the expected benefits of ISO IEC 27002 to the stakeholder?
<--- Score

46. What activities does the governance board need to consider?
<--- Score

47. Looking at each person individually – does every one have the qualities which are needed to work in this group?
<--- Score

48. Do you clarify your resilience and recovery needs and requirements?
<--- Score

49. Do you clarify what must be done when problems are discovered?
<--- Score

50. What is the smallest subset of the problem you can usefully solve?
<--- Score

51. How much are sponsors, customers, partners, stakeholders involved in ISO IEC 27002? In other words, what are the risks, if ISO IEC 27002 does not deliver successfully?
<--- Score

52. Will new equipment/products be required to facilitate ISO IEC 27002 delivery, for example is new software needed?
<--- Score

53. How are you going to measure success?
<--- Score

54. Have you identified your ISO IEC 27002 key performance indicators?
<--- Score

55. How does it fit into your organizational needs and tasks?
<--- Score

56. Do you need to avoid or amend any ISO IEC 27002 activities?
<--- Score

57. Do you ask them to identify critical product

and service components?
<--- Score

58. Do you ask them to share information about potential problems?
<--- Score

59. What is important and needs protecting?
<--- Score

60. Have you identified all of the information security requirements that you expect suppliers to comply with?
<--- Score

61. Do you consider the need to be accountable for actions and inactions?
<--- Score

62. Who else hopes to benefit from it?
<--- Score

63. Does your organization need more ISO IEC 27002 education?
<--- Score

64. To what extent would your organization benefit from being recognized as a award recipient?
<--- Score

Add up total points for this section:
_ _ _ _ _ = Total points for this section

Divided by: _ _ _ _ _ _ (number of statements answered) = _ _ _ _ _ _
Average score for this section

Transfer your score to the ISO IEC 27002
Index at the beginning of the Self-
Assessment.

CRITERION #2: DEFINE:

INTENT: Formulate the stakeholder problem. Define the problem, needs and objectives.

In my belief, the answer to this question is clearly defined:

5 Strongly Agree

4 Agree

3 Neutral

2 Disagree

1 Strongly Disagree

1. How are the metrics defined in detail?
<--- Score

2. Is ISO IEC 27002 required?
<--- Score

3. What specifically is the problem? Where does it occur? When does it occur? What is its extent?
<--- Score

4. What are the Roles and Responsibilities for each team member and its leadership? Where is this documented?
<--- Score

5. What are the rough order estimates on cost savings/ opportunities that ISO IEC 27002 brings?
<--- Score

6. Does the team have regular meetings?
<--- Score

7. Do you clarify information security requirements whenever your suppliers must provide it infrastructure components?
<--- Score

8. Do you describe your security training and awareness requirements?
<--- Score

9. Who are the ISO IEC 27002 improvement team members, including Management Leads and Coaches?
<--- Score

10. Are assessments or effectiveness metrics required?
<--- Score

11. What constraints exist that might impact the team?
<--- Score

12. Have you defined information security

responsibilities and duties that remain valid after personnel are terminated or responsibilities change?
<--- Score

13. Are required metrics defined, what are they?
<--- Score

14. Why are you doing ISO IEC 27002 and what is the scope?
<--- Score

15. Are there different segments of customers?
<--- Score

16. Is full participation by members in regularly held team meetings guaranteed?
<--- Score

17. Has a project plan, Gantt chart, or similar been developed/completed?
<--- Score

18. How are use cases defined and based on what?
<--- Score

19. Do you clarify requirements for information products and services?
<--- Score

20. Is there a ISO IEC 27002 management charter, including stakeholder case, problem and goal statements, scope, milestones, roles and responsibilities, communication plan?
<--- Score

21. Has a team charter been developed and communicated?
<--- Score

22. Do you make sure that your managers require all contractors to apply your organizations information security policies and procedures?
<--- Score

23. Will team members regularly document their ISO IEC 27002 work?
<--- Score

24. Do you expect them to see if services meet security requirements?
<--- Score

25. Do you expect them to see if products meet security requirements?
<--- Score

26. How do you gather ISO IEC 27002 requirements?
<--- Score

27. How did the ISO IEC 27002 manager receive input to the development of a ISO IEC 27002 improvement plan and the estimated completion dates/times of each activity?
<--- Score

28. Do you describe intellectual property rights and requirements?
<--- Score

29. What is in the scope and what is not in scope?
<--- Score

30. Has the direction changed at all during the course of ISO IEC 27002? If so, when did it change and why?
<--- Score

31. Do you account for how legal and regulatory requirements must be met?
<--- Score

32. Do you make sure that your managers require all employees to apply your organizations information security policies and procedures?
<--- Score

33. What would be the goal or target for a ISO IEC 27002's improvement team?
<--- Score

34. Do you expect your suppliers to comply with all security requirements?
<--- Score

35. Do you expect them to ensure that services meet requirements?
<--- Score

36. Is there a critical path to deliver ISO IEC 27002 results?
<--- Score

37. Who defines (or who defined) the rules and roles?
<--- Score

38. Is there regularly 100% attendance at the team meetings? If not, have appointed substitutes attended to preserve cross-functionality and full

representation?

<--- Score

39. Do you ask suppliers to propagate required security practices?

<--- Score

40. Is the team equipped with available and reliable resources?

<--- Score

41. Prescriptive - are the framework control requirements sufficiently detailed to reduce ambiguity in implementation?

<--- Score

42. How do you keep key subject matter experts in the loop?

<--- Score

43. Is there a completed SIPOC representation, describing the Suppliers, Inputs, Process, Outputs, and Customers?

<--- Score

44. How do you manage changes in ISO IEC 27002 requirements?

<--- Score

45. How are use cases structured?

<--- Score

46. Do you clarify information security requirements whenever suppliers must access your organizations information?

<--- Score

47. Is ISO IEC 27002 linked to key stakeholder goals and objectives?
<--- Score

48. What is out of scope?
<--- Score

49. How is the team tracking and documenting its work?
<--- Score

50. What are the legal requirements for breach notification?
<--- Score

51. Did you define how background verifications should be performed?
<--- Score

52. Are customer(s) identified and segmented according to their different needs and requirements?
<--- Score

53. Did you define security requirements for each type of information?
<--- Score

54. Did you define background verification criteria and clarify limitations?
<--- Score

55. Are audit criteria, scope, frequency and methods defined?
<--- Score

56. What is the definition of success?
<--- Score

57. Do you clarify employment contract requirements that remain valid?
<--- Score

58. Has anyone else (internal or external to the group) attempted to solve this problem or a similar one before? If so, what knowledge can be leveraged from these previous efforts?
<--- Score

59. When are meeting minutes sent out? Who is on the distribution list?
<--- Score

60. Do you describe your organizations incident management requirements?
<--- Score

61. Do you enforce your organizations post-employment information security expectations and requirements?
<--- Score

62. Has the improvement team collected the 'voice of the customer' (obtained feedback – qualitative and quantitative)?
<--- Score

63. What are the record-keeping requirements of ISO IEC 27002 activities?
<--- Score

64. Is ISO IEC 27002 currently on schedule according

to the plan?
<--- Score

65. Do you clarify information security requirements whenever suppliers must communicate using your organizations information?
<--- Score

66. Do you define security requirements that apply to your suppliers?
<--- Score

67. Do you clarify requirements for communications technologies?
<--- Score

68. How do you think the partners involved in ISO IEC 27002 would have defined success?
<--- Score

69. What are the ISO IEC 27002 use cases?
<--- Score

70. Do you specify personnel screening requirements and responsibilities?
<--- Score

71. Do you communicate your post-employment information security requirements to both employees and contractors?
<--- Score

72. What customer feedback methods were used to solicit their input?
<--- Score

73. How do you catch ISO IEC 27002 definition inconsistencies?
<--- Score

74. What is the worst case scenario?
<--- Score

75. Is the team adequately staffed with the desired cross-functionality? If not, what additional resources are available to the team?
<--- Score

76. Is the current 'as is' process being followed? If not, what are the discrepancies?
<--- Score

77. What are the compelling stakeholder reasons for embarking on ISO IEC 27002?
<--- Score

78. What baselines are required to be defined and managed?
<--- Score

79. What are the dynamics of the communication plan?
<--- Score

80. Do you review compliance with information security requirements?
<--- Score

81. Do you clarify the requirements that your suppliers suppliers must meet?
<--- Score

82. Have the customer needs been translated into specific, measurable requirements? How?
<--- Score

83. What are the boundaries of the scope? What is in bounds and what is not? What is the start point? What is the stop point?
<--- Score

84. Do you clarify what happens if security requirements are disregarded?
<--- Score

85. Has a high-level 'as is' process map been completed, verified and validated?
<--- Score

86. Are there any constraints known that bear on the ability to perform ISO IEC 27002 work? How is the team addressing them?
<--- Score

87. Do you define and implement use cases?
<--- Score

88. Do you ask suppliers to propagate security requirements?
<--- Score

89. How often are the team meetings?
<--- Score

90. Do you inform candidates beforehand when legally required?
<--- Score

91. Has the ISO IEC 27002 work been fairly and/
or equitably divided and delegated among team
members who are qualified and capable to perform
the work? Has everyone contributed?
<--- Score

92. What defines best in class?
<--- Score

**93. Do you define the security requirements that
suppliers must meet?**
<--- Score

94. Is there any additional ISO IEC 27002 definition of
success?
<--- Score

**95. Do you clarify how long security requirements
are valid?**
<--- Score

96. What critical content must be communicated –
who, what, when, where, and how?
<--- Score

97. How will variation in the actual durations of each
activity be dealt with to ensure that the expected ISO
IEC 27002 results are met?
<--- Score

98. Has a ISO IEC 27002 requirement not been met?
<--- Score

99. When is/was the ISO IEC 27002 start date?
<--- Score

100. Did the business or management provide any requirements?
<--- Score

101. Is the ISO IEC 27002 scope manageable?
<--- Score

102. How does the ISO IEC 27002 manager ensure against scope creep?
<--- Score

103. What is the definition of ISO IEC 27002 excellence?
<--- Score

104. Has/have the customer(s) been identified?
<--- Score

105. What is the scope of ISO IEC 27002?
<--- Score

106. How was the 'as is' process map developed, reviewed, verified and validated?
<--- Score

107. Is there a completed, verified, and validated high-level 'as is' (not 'should be' or 'could be') stakeholder process map?
<--- Score

108. Do the problem and goal statements meet the SMART criteria (specific, measurable, attainable, relevant, and time-bound)?
<--- Score

109. Are different versions of process maps needed to account for the different types of inputs?
<--- Score

110. Do you expect them to ensure that products meet requirements?
<--- Score

111. Do you describe all relevant legal and regulatory requirements?
<--- Score

112. How will the ISO IEC 27002 team and the group measure complete success of ISO IEC 27002?
<--- Score

113. Are applicable to your ISMS, and which are irrelevant, not appropriate or otherwise not required?
<--- Score

114. What key stakeholder process output measure(s) does ISO IEC 27002 leverage and how?
<--- Score

115. Is data collected and displayed to better understand customer(s) critical needs and requirements.
<--- Score

116. Do you define access controls for each type of information?
<--- Score

117. Are resources adequate for the scope?
<--- Score

118. What ISO IEC 27002 services do you require?
<--- Score

119. Do you consider legal obligations and contractual requirements?
<--- Score

120. Where can you gather more information?
<--- Score

121. How are use cases maintained?
<--- Score

122. Do you define the requirements that apply to suppliers purchases?
<--- Score

123. Will a ISO IEC 27002 production readiness review be required?
<--- Score

124. Has everyone on the team, including the team leaders, been properly trained?
<--- Score

125. Have all basic functions of ISO IEC 27002 been defined?
<--- Score

126. Is the improvement team aware of the different versions of a process: what they think it is vs. what it actually is vs. what it should be vs. what it could be?
<--- Score

127. If substitutes have been appointed, have they

been briefed on the ISO IEC 27002 goals and received regular communications as to the progress to date?
<--- Score

128. Will team members perform ISO IEC 27002 work when assigned and in a timely fashion?
<--- Score

129. Are specialized siem skills defined?
<--- Score

130. Is it clearly defined in and to your organization what you do?
<--- Score

131. Do you define your minimum information security requirements?
<--- Score

132. When is the estimated completion date?
<--- Score

133. Do you have a ISO IEC 27002 success story or case study ready to tell and share?
<--- Score

134. Do you clarify confidentiality requirements that remain valid?
<--- Score

135. Do you clarify nondisclosure requirements that remain valid?
<--- Score

136. Do you clarify information security requirements whenever suppliers must store your

organizations information?

<--- Score

Add up total points for this section:
_ _ _ _ _ = Total points for this section

Divided by: _ _ _ _ _ _ (number of
statements answered) = _ _ _ _ _ _
Average score for this section

Transfer your score to the ISO IEC 27002
Index at the beginning of the Self-
Assessment.

CRITERION #3: MEASURE:

INTENT: Gather the correct data. Measure the current performance and evolution of the situation.

In my belief, the answer to this question is clearly defined:

5 Strongly Agree

4 Agree

3 Neutral

2 Disagree

1 Strongly Disagree

1. When should you bother with diagrams?
<--- Score

2. What causes mismanagement?
<--- Score

3. Is data collected on key measures that were identified?
<--- Score

4. What is the total cost related to deploying ISO IEC 27002, including any consulting or professional services?
<--- Score

5. What relevant entities could be measured?
<--- Score

6. Is Process Variation Displayed/Communicated?
<--- Score

7. How are you verifying it?
<--- Score

8. Do you verify the candidates curriculum vitae (résumé)?
<--- Score

9. Is the scope of ISO IEC 27002 cost analysis cost-effective?
<--- Score

10. What would be a real cause for concern?
<--- Score

11. What are focus areas of SIEM and how do IT risk frameworks address them?
<--- Score

12. How do you quantify and qualify impacts?
<--- Score

13. Are actual costs in line with budgeted costs?
<--- Score

14. What are allowable costs?
<--- Score

15. Are high impact defects defined and identified in the stakeholder process?
<--- Score

16. Have you made assumptions about the shape of the future, particularly its impact on your customers and competitors?
<--- Score

17. Where do you focus with respect to supply chain risk management?
<--- Score

18. What are the estimated costs of proposed changes?
<--- Score

19. How large is the gap between current performance and the customer-specified (goal) performance?
<--- Score

20. Who should receive measurement reports?
<--- Score

21. Have you found any 'ground fruit' or 'low-hanging fruit' for immediate remedies to the gap in performance?
<--- Score

22. Is long term and short term variability accounted for?
<--- Score

23. Do you verify that security incidents and issues are well managed?
<--- Score

24. How will success or failure be measured?
<--- Score

25. Who is involved in verifying compliance?
<--- Score

26. Is the solution cost-effective?
<--- Score

27. Do you verify candidates occupational qualifications?
<--- Score

28. Do you verify candidates qualifications?
<--- Score

29. Do you arrange regular progress meetings (to verify compliance)?
<--- Score

30. Are key measures identified and agreed upon?
<--- Score

31. When is Root Cause Analysis Required?
<--- Score

32. What is the total fixed cost?
<--- Score

33. How do you measure efficient delivery of ISO IEC 27002 services?

<--- Score

34. What data was collected (past, present, future/ongoing)?
<--- Score

35. What particular quality tools did the team find helpful in establishing measurements?
<--- Score

36. How do you know that any ISO IEC 27002 analysis is complete and comprehensive?
<--- Score

37. The approach of traditional ISO IEC 27002 works for detail complexity but is focused on a systematic approach rather than an understanding of the nature of systems themselves, what approach will permit your organization to deal with the kind of unpredictable emergent behaviors that dynamic complexity can introduce?
<--- Score

38. How do you measure success?
<--- Score

39. Do you verify that services can be provided after big disasters?
<--- Score

40. Is it possible to estimate the impact of unanticipated complexity such as wrong or failed assumptions, feedback, etcetera on proposed reforms?
<--- Score

41. Does ISO IEC 27002 analysis isolate the fundamental causes of problems?
<--- Score

42. Do you verify that corrective actions were taken?
<--- Score

43. Which measures and indicators matter?
<--- Score

44. What tests verify requirements?
<--- Score

45. What causes investor action?
<--- Score

46. How do your measurements capture actionable ISO IEC 27002 information for use in exceeding your customers expectations and securing your customers engagement?
<--- Score

47. How do you verify the authenticity of the data and information used?
<--- Score

48. When are costs are incurred?
<--- Score

49. Are losses documented, analyzed, and remedial processes developed to prevent future losses?
<--- Score

50. Are process variation components displayed/ communicated using suitable charts, graphs, plots?
<--- Score

51. What are the agreed upon definitions of the high impact areas, defect(s), unit(s), and opportunities that will figure into the process capability metrics?
<--- Score

52. What charts has the team used to display the components of variation in the process?
<--- Score

53. What causes extra work or rework?
<--- Score

54. What are the uncertainties surrounding estimates of impact?
<--- Score

55. Do you consider the impact security breaches have on business?
<--- Score

56. What has the team done to assure the stability and accuracy of the measurement process?
<--- Score

57. What are the key input variables? What are the key process variables? What are the key output variables?
<--- Score

58. How does cost-to-serve analysis help?
<--- Score

59. Did you perform a threat-actor analysis?
<--- Score

60. What key measures identified indicate the

performance of the stakeholder process?
<--- Score

61. How do you aggregate measures across priorities?
<--- Score

62. What are the ISO IEC 27002 key cost drivers?
<--- Score

63. How do you verify if ISO IEC 27002 is built right?
<--- Score

64. How are costs allocated?
<--- Score

65. How will costs be allocated?
<--- Score

66. Do you verify the candidates academic qualifications?
<--- Score

67. What is your ISO IEC 27002 quality cost segregation study?
<--- Score

68. What disadvantage does this cause for the user?
<--- Score

69. Do you aggressively reward and promote the people who have the biggest impact on creating excellent ISO IEC 27002 services/products?
<--- Score

70. What measurements are possible, practicable and meaningful?

<--- Score

71. Did you tackle the cause or the symptom?
<--- Score

72. How do you stay flexible and focused to recognize larger ISO IEC 27002 results?
<--- Score

73. When were measurements conducted, and by whom?
<--- Score

74. What are your operating costs?
<--- Score

75. Are the units of measure consistent?
<--- Score

76. Do you verify candidates academic qualifications?
<--- Score

77. How is performance measured?
<--- Score

78. How will your organization measure success?
<--- Score

79. Do you teach people about your password security measures?
<--- Score

80. Is a solid data collection plan established that includes measurement systems analysis?
<--- Score

81. Are missed ISO IEC 27002 opportunities costing your organization money?
<--- Score

82. Do you verify the trustworthiness of information security candidates?
<--- Score

83. Do you verify that suppliers are capable of maintaining service levels?
<--- Score

84. Is there a Performance Baseline?
<--- Score

85. Have the types of risks that may impact ISO IEC 27002 been identified and analyzed?
<--- Score

86. How do you verify ISO IEC 27002 completeness and accuracy?
<--- Score

87. Can you do ISO IEC 27002 without complex (expensive) analysis?
<--- Score

88. What does your operating model cost?
<--- Score

89. What are your customers expectations and measures?
<--- Score

90. Was a data collection plan established?

<--- Score

91. When a disaster occurs, who gets priority?
<--- Score

92. Do the benefits outweigh the costs?
<--- Score

93. Is key measure data collection planned
and executed, process variation displayed and
communicated and performance baselined?
<--- Score

**94. Do you verify the competence of information
security candidates?**
<--- Score

95. Have you included everything in your ISO IEC
27002 cost models?
<--- Score

96. What is your cost benefit analysis?
<--- Score

**97. Do you verify the candidates occupational
qualifications?**
<--- Score

98. What are the operational costs after ISO IEC 27002
deployment?
<--- Score

99. Is data collection planned and executed?
<--- Score

100. What are you verifying?

<--- Score

101. What is an unallowable cost?
<--- Score

102. Are there any easy-to-implement alternatives to ISO IEC 27002? Sometimes other solutions are available that do not require the cost implications of a full-blown project?
<--- Score

103. What does a Test Case verify?
<--- Score

104. Do you verify that acceptable service levels can be maintained?
<--- Score

105. How sensitive must the ISO IEC 27002 strategy be to cost?
<--- Score

106. Who participated in the data collection for measurements?
<--- Score

107. How do you verify ISO IEC 27002 completeness and accuracy?
<--- Score

108. Are you able to realize any cost savings?
<--- Score

109. What is your decision requirements diagram?
<--- Score

110. Do you verify the professional history of all candidates?

<--- Score

Add up total points for this section:
_____ = Total points for this section

Divided by: _____ (number of statements answered) = _____
Average score for this section

Transfer your score to the ISO IEC 27002 Index at the beginning of the Self-Assessment.

CRITERION #4: ANALYZE:

INTENT: Analyze causes, assumptions and hypotheses.

In my belief, the answer to this question is clearly defined:

5 Strongly Agree

4 Agree

3 Neutral

2 Disagree

1 Strongly Disagree

1. Do your leaders quickly bounce back from setbacks?
<--- Score

2. Do you collect evidence before you initiate a disciplinary process?
<--- Score

3. What were the financial benefits resulting from any 'ground fruit or low-hanging fruit' (quick fixes)?

<--- Score

4. Which factor is not important for determining the value of data for your organization?
<--- Score

5. Is the required ISO IEC 27002 data gathered?
<--- Score

6. What are your ISO IEC 27002 processes?
<--- Score

7. Have you established a process to manage your relationship with suppliers?
<--- Score

8. Do you clarify information security requirements whenever suppliers must process your organizations information?
<--- Score

9. Do others ensure that people have the right skills and qualifications?
<--- Score

10. What process should you select for improvement?
<--- Score

11. Is the ISO IEC 27002 process severely broken such that a re-design is necessary?
<--- Score

12. What were the crucial 'moments of truth' on the process map?
<--- Score

13. What tools were used to generate the list of possible causes?
<--- Score

14. How do you implement and manage your work processes to ensure that they meet design requirements?
<--- Score

15. Are gaps between current performance and the goal performance identified?
<--- Score

16. How do you ensure that your data does not leave the country?
<--- Score

17. Do you use your disciplinary process to deter future security breaches?
<--- Score

18. Were Pareto charts (or similar) used to portray the 'heavy hitters' (or key sources of variation)?
<--- Score

19. Did you establish third party review processes and procedures?
<--- Score

20. Do you think about how critical your business information is and how important your systems and processes are whenever you evaluate changes to supplier services?
<--- Score

21. Do you ask suppliers to create a process to

identify critical components?
<--- Score

22. What does the data say about the performance of the stakeholder process?
<--- Score

23. Is the suppliers process defined and controlled?
<--- Score

24. What methods do you use to gather ISO IEC 27002 data?
<--- Score

25. What are the revised rough estimates of the financial savings/opportunity for ISO IEC 27002 improvements?
<--- Score

26. A compounding model resolution with available relevant data can often provide insight towards a solution methodology; which ISO IEC 27002 models, tools and techniques are necessary?
<--- Score

27. What successful thing are you doing today that may be blinding you to new growth opportunities?
<--- Score

28. What qualifications and skills do you need?
<--- Score

29. Have any additional benefits been identified that will result from closing all or most of the gaps?
<--- Score

30. What qualifications are needed?
<--- Score

31. Was a detailed process map created to amplify critical steps of the 'as is' stakeholder process?
<--- Score

32. Is the performance gap determined?
<--- Score

33. What other organizational variables, such as reward systems or communication systems, affect the performance of this ISO IEC 27002 process?
<--- Score

34. Did you establish processes and procedures for each type of supplier?
<--- Score

35. Did you establish product validation processes and procedures?
<--- Score

36. What conclusions were drawn from the team's data collection and analysis? How did the team reach these conclusions?
<--- Score

37. What type of proof do you want that data have been destroyed?
<--- Score

38. Did you design a graduated process that requires a measured response?
<--- Score

39. How do mission and objectives affect the ISO IEC 27002 processes of your organization?
<--- Score

40. Is data and process analysis, root cause analysis and quantifying the gap/opportunity in place?
<--- Score

41. Do you communicate your disciplinary process and make sure that all employees are aware of what happens when security is breached?
<--- Score

42. Do you teach buyers about your policies, processes and procedures?
<--- Score

43. Were any designed experiments used to generate additional insight into the data analysis?
<--- Score

44. Do you describe your right to audit suppliers processes and controls?
<--- Score

45. What quality tools were used to get through the analyze phase?
<--- Score

46. Do you clarify how information processing facilities are protected?
<--- Score

47. Do you control how suppliers process sensitive information?
<--- Score

48. Has data output been validated?
<--- Score

49. Did you establish processes and procedures for each type of access?
<--- Score

50. Do you use them to ensure the integrity of information processing?
<--- Score

51. What are your key performance measures or indicators and in-process measures for the control and improvement of your ISO IEC 27002 processes?
<--- Score

52. What third-party products are used for processing?
<--- Score

53. What is the cost of poor quality as supported by the team's analysis?
<--- Score

54. Do you apply your disciplinary process whenever a breach occurs?
<--- Score

55. Has an output goal been set?
<--- Score

56. Have you established a process for screening contractors?
<--- Score

57. Is the gap/opportunity displayed and communicated in financial terms?
<--- Score

58. Do you describe data protection obligations and requirements?
<--- Score

59. How is ISO IEC 27002 data gathered?
<--- Score

60. Have you established a formal disciplinary process to handle employees who have committed a security breach?
<--- Score

61. Are your outputs consistent?
<--- Score

62. Do you clarify specific duties during the pre-employment process?
<--- Score

63. Do you ensure that people have the right skills and qualifications?
<--- Score

64. Identify an operational issue in your organization, for example, could a particular task be done more quickly or more efficiently by ISO IEC 27002?
<--- Score

65. Have the problem and goal statements been updated to reflect the additional knowledge gained from the analyze phase?
<--- Score

66. Do you have the authority to produce the output?
<--- Score

67. Are all team members qualified for all tasks?
<--- Score

68. How is the data gathered?
<--- Score

69. How has the ISO IEC 27002 data been gathered?
<--- Score

70. Do you develop processes and procedures that suppliers must use?
<--- Score

71. Was a cause-and-effect diagram used to explore the different types of causes (or sources of variation)?
<--- Score

72. Do you describe defect resolution and conflict resolution processes?
<--- Score

73. Did you establish a security incident reporting process?
<--- Score

74. Did you develop a typical supplier relationship management process?
<--- Score

75. What tools were used to narrow the list of possible causes?
<--- Score

76. What are the necessary qualifications?
<--- Score

77. Do you use your process to share information about security incidents?
<--- Score

78. What are your outputs?
<--- Score

79. Do you ensure that information processing facilities are safeguarded?
<--- Score

80. Are ISO IEC 27002 changes recognized early enough to be approved through the regular process?
<--- Score

81. Do you establish control by developing processes and procedures?
<--- Score

82. Where do you describe your right to audit suppliers processes and controls?
<--- Score

83. Did any value-added analysis or 'lean thinking' take place to identify some of the gaps shown on the 'as is' process map?
<--- Score

84. What is the output?
<--- Score

85. Did any additional data need to be collected?

<--- Score

86. Do you use your process to coordinate and control critical suppliers?
<--- Score

87. How was the detailed process map generated, verified, and validated?
<--- Score

88. Did you implement your supplier relationship management process?
<--- Score

89. What processes and assets need protection?
<--- Score

90. Do you use your process to ensure that suppliers can provide services?
<--- Score

91. Did you design a process that treats offenders fairly and correctly?
<--- Score

92. What did the team gain from developing a sub-process map?
<--- Score

93. How do you promote understanding that opportunity for improvement is not criticism of the status quo, or the people who created the status quo?
<--- Score

94. Were there any improvement opportunities identified from the process analysis?

<--- Score

95. Do you develop processes and procedures that you must apply?
<--- Score

96. Where is the data coming from to measure compliance?
<--- Score

97. What are the best opportunities for value improvement?
<--- Score

98. Do you clarify copyright and data protection laws?
<--- Score

99. Do you check more if information processing facilities will be accessed?
<--- Score

100. Do you use suppliers to ensure the integrity of information processing?
<--- Score

101. Did you design a formal disciplinary process to handle security breaches?
<--- Score

Add up total points for this section:
_ _ _ _ _ = Total points for this section

Divided by: _ _ _ _ _ _ (number of statements answered) = _ _ _ _ _ _
Average score for this section

Transfer your score to the ISO IEC 27002
Index at the beginning of the Self-
Assessment.

CRITERION #5: IMPROVE:

INTENT: Develop a practical solution.
Innovate, establish and test the
solution and to measure the results.

In my belief, the answer to this
question is clearly defined:

5 Strongly Agree

4 Agree

3 Neutral

2 Disagree

1 Strongly Disagree

1. Did you develop information security agreements for each supplier?
<--- Score

2. Is the solution technically practical?
<--- Score

3. Are improved process ('should be') maps modified based on pilot data and analysis?

<--- Score

4. What does the 'should be' process map/design look like?
<--- Score

5. What were the underlying assumptions on the cost-benefit analysis?
<--- Score

6. Are possible solutions generated and tested?
<--- Score

7. Do you document the security agreements you have with each supplier?
<--- Score

8. What lessons, if any, from a pilot were incorporated into the design of the full-scale solution?
<--- Score

9. Do you manage and control the development of new applications?
<--- Score

10. How are policy decisions made and where?
<--- Score

11. What tools were used to tap into the creativity and encourage 'outside the box' thinking?
<--- Score

12. Do you make sure that background verifications take your unique security risks and requirements into consideration?
<--- Score

13. What is the risk?
<--- Score

14. How do you link measurement and risk?
<--- Score

15. What went well, what should change, what can improve?
<--- Score

16. Was a ISO IEC 27002 charter developed?
<--- Score

17. How does the solution remove the key sources of issues discovered in the analyze phase?
<--- Score

18. Were any criteria developed to assist the team in testing and evaluating potential solutions?
<--- Score

19. Do you perform more rigorous background verification checks whenever the perceived security risk is greater?
<--- Score

20. Do you manage and control the use of new development environments?
<--- Score

21. Do you clarify the information security risks that exist whenever your suppliers have access to your organizations assets?
<--- Score

22. Describe the design of the pilot and what tests were conducted, if any?
<--- Score

23. Do you evaluate supplier service delivery and compliance?
<--- Score

24. Are new and improved process ('should be') maps developed?
<--- Score

25. Do you manage and control the development of new systems?
<--- Score

26. Do you manage and control the use of new development tools?
<--- Score

27. Are you assessing ISO IEC 27002 and risk?
<--- Score

28. What is the ISO IEC 27002's sustainability risk?
<--- Score

29. Do you consider your unique risk profile and business needs?
<--- Score

30. How are risks identified and assessed?
<--- Score

31. What can you do to improve?
<--- Score

32. Is supporting ISO IEC 27002 documentation required?
<--- Score

33. Do you use your supplier access policy to document your access controls?
<--- Score

34. Do you expect your suppliers to address the information security risks connected with use of information and communications technology services and product supply chains?
<--- Score

35. Who controls the risk?
<--- Score

36. Do you evaluate changes to services provided by your suppliers?
<--- Score

37. Are risk triggers captured?
<--- Score

38. Which of the recognised risks out of all risks can be most likely transferred?
<--- Score

39. Do you manage and control all attempts to improve security?
<--- Score

40. What attendant changes will need to be made to ensure that the solution is successful?
<--- Score

41. Are there any constraints (technical, political, cultural, or otherwise) that would inhibit certain solutions?
<--- Score

42. Are the best solutions selected?
<--- Score

43. Did you develop a typical supplier relationship management lifecycle?
<--- Score

44. Do you document all information security requirements and controls?
<--- Score

45. How are risks documented?
<--- Score

46. To what extent does management recognize ISO IEC 27002 as a tool to increase the results?
<--- Score

47. Do you ask suppliers to help you manage related security risks?
<--- Score

48. Is there a cost/benefit analysis of optimal solution(s)?
<--- Score

49. What communications are necessary to support the implementation of the solution?
<--- Score

50. Where does your organization locate the cyber

security risk management program/office?
<--- Score

51. How risky is your organization?
<--- Score

52. What actually has to improve and by how much?
<--- Score

53. Is a solution implementation plan established, including schedule/work breakdown structure, resources, risk management plan, cost/budget, and control plan?
<--- Score

54. Do you clarify your risk mitigation requirements and the risk mitigation expectations that your organizations suppliers must comply with?
<--- Score

55. Who will be using the results of the measurement activities?
<--- Score

56. ISO IEC 27002 risk decisions: whose call Is It?
<--- Score

57. Is pilot data collected and analyzed?
<--- Score

58. Do you cover the five essential competencies: Communication, Collaboration,Innovation, Adaptability, and Leadership that improve an organizations ability to leverage the new ISO IEC 27002 in a volatile global economy?

<--- Score

59. How will the group know that the solution worked?
<--- Score

60. How do you improve your likelihood of success ?
<--- Score

61. Is the optimal solution selected based on testing and analysis?
<--- Score

62. Who will be responsible for making the decisions to include or exclude requested changes once ISO IEC 27002 is underway?
<--- Score

63. Do you document your security risk mitigation agreements?
<--- Score

64. How will you know that you have improved?
<--- Score

65. What is the implementation plan?
<--- Score

66. Do you regularly evaluate your information security awareness program?
<--- Score

67. Is there a small-scale pilot for proposed improvement(s)? What conclusions were drawn from the outcomes of a pilot?
<--- Score

68. How do you define the solutions' scope?
<--- Score

69. How do you measure improved ISO IEC 27002 service perception, and satisfaction?
<--- Score

70. What error proofing will be done to address some of the discrepancies observed in the 'as is' process?
<--- Score

71. Do you expect your suppliers to control own supply chain risks?
<--- Score

72. What are the underlying conceptual models used in Risk Assessment frameworks?
<--- Score

73. How do you manage and improve your ISO IEC 27002 work systems to deliver customer value and achieve organizational success and sustainability?
<--- Score

74. What needs improvement? Why?
<--- Score

75. Is the implementation plan designed?
<--- Score

76. What do you want to improve?
<--- Score

77. Was a pilot designed for the proposed solution(s)?
<--- Score

78. What tools were most useful during the improve phase?
<--- Score

79. For estimation problems, how do you develop an estimation statement?
<--- Score

80. What is the magnitude of the improvements?
<--- Score

81. How can skill-level changes improve ISO IEC 27002?
<--- Score

82. How will the team or the process owner(s) monitor the implementation plan to see that it is working as intended?
<--- Score

83. How did the team generate the list of possible solutions?
<--- Score

84. What is ISO IEC 27002's impact on utilizing the best solution(s)?
<--- Score

85. Do you document the security obligations that your suppliers have?
<--- Score

86. Do you re-assess your organizations information security risks whenever changes to supplier services are being considered?

<--- Score

87. Are decisions made in a timely manner?
<--- Score

88. What tools were used to evaluate the potential solutions?
<--- Score

89. Do you include information security risk management requirements in the agreements you have with your organizations suppliers?
<--- Score

90. How can you improve ISO IEC 27002?
<--- Score

91. How can you improve performance?
<--- Score

92. Do you establish security risk mitigation agreements with suppliers?
<--- Score

93. Can the solution be designed and implemented within an acceptable time period?
<--- Score

94. What is the team's contingency plan for potential problems occurring in implementation?
<--- Score

95. Is a contingency plan established?
<--- Score

96. How do you keep improving ISO IEC 27002?

<--- Score

97. How is the ISO IEC 27002 Value Stream Mapping managed?
<--- Score

98. If you could go back in time five years, what decision would you make differently? What is your best guess as to what decision you're making today you might regret five years from now?
<--- Score

99. How do risks develop?
<--- Score

100. When you map the key players in your own work and the types/domains of relationships with them, which relationships do you find easy and which challenging, and why?
<--- Score

101. Do you evaluate your information security awareness program?
<--- Score

Add up total points for this section:
_ _ _ _ _ = Total points for this section

Divided by: _ _ _ _ _ _ (number of statements answered) = _ _ _ _ _ _
Average score for this section

Transfer your score to the ISO IEC 27002 Index at the beginning of the Self-Assessment.

CRITERION #6: CONTROL:

INTENT: Implement the practical solution. Maintain the performance and correct possible complications.

In my belief, the answer to this question is clearly defined:

5 Strongly Agree

4 Agree

3 Neutral

2 Disagree

1 Strongly Disagree

1. Have new or revised work instructions resulted?
<--- Score

2. Do you manage and control changes in the use of subcontractors?
<--- Score

3. Is new knowledge gained imbedded in the response plan?

<--- Score

4. Do you teach people about your malware control mechanisms?

<--- Score

5. Are you measuring, monitoring and predicting ISO IEC 27002 activities to optimize operations and profitability, and enhancing outcomes?
<--- Score

6. How might the group capture best practices and lessons learned so as to leverage improvements?
<--- Score

7. Did you think about newly adopted information security controls?

<--- Score

8. How will report readings be checked to effectively monitor performance?
<--- Score

9. Is a response plan in place for when the input, process, or output measures indicate an 'out-of-control' condition?
<--- Score

10. How will input, process, and output variables be checked to detect for sub-optimal conditions?
<--- Score

11. Do you monitor how critical suppliers manage your security?

<--- Score

12. Does your organization have a methodology in place for the proper allocation of business resources to invest in, create, and maintain it standards?

<--- Score

13. Did you consider using web-based learning methods?

<--- Score

14. Do you expect suppliers to establish a supplier monitoring process?

<--- Score

15. Do you monitor supplier service delivery and information security?

<--- Score

16. Do you control how suppliers subcontract to another supplier?

<--- Score

17. What quality tools were useful in the control phase?

<--- Score

18. Do you use your controls to ensure the integrity of information?

<--- Score

19. Is there documentation that will support the successful operation of the improvement?

<--- Score

20. Do you monitor how suppliers protect sensitive information?

<--- Score

21. Do you monitor suppliers service delivery performance levels?
<--- Score

22. Did you establish controls to restrict supplier access to your information?
<--- Score

23. Does the ISO IEC 27002 performance meet the customer's requirements?
<--- Score

24. Do you monitor how suppliers process sensitive information?
<--- Score

25. Do you monitor the effectiveness of your ISO IEC 27002 activities?
<--- Score

26. What other controls may assist?
<--- Score

27. Do you map your organizations scheme against each suppliers?
<--- Score

28. What other areas of the group might benefit from the ISO IEC 27002 team's improvements, knowledge, and learning?
<--- Score

29. Do you make your personnel aware of your supplier access controls?

<--- Score

30. Do you describe the access controls that must be established?
<--- Score

31. Do you use your process to monitor supplier service and compliance?
<--- Score

32. Do you control how suppliers access sensitive information?
<--- Score

33. Do you describe how you plan to monitor supplier performance?
<--- Score

34. How do you encourage people to take control and responsibility?
<--- Score

35. Did you consider using self-paced learning methods?
<--- Score

36. Are suggested corrective/restorative actions indicated on the response plan for known causes to problems that might surface?
<--- Score

37. What do you stand for--and what are you against?
<--- Score

38. Do you expect managers to support policies, procedures, and controls?

<--- Score

39. Who sets the ISO IEC 27002 standards?
<--- Score

40. Did you design and plan an information security awareness program?
<--- Score

41. How will ISO IEC 27002 decisions be made and monitored?
<--- Score

42. Is there a documented and implemented monitoring plan?
<--- Score

43. What are the critical parameters to watch?
<--- Score

44. Do you monitor the ISO IEC 27002 decisions made and fine tune them as they evolve?
<--- Score

45. Do you manage and control changes in location or service facilities?
<--- Score

46. Do you describe how transitions should be managed and controlled?
<--- Score

47. Is knowledge gained on process shared and institutionalized?
<--- Score

48. Did you describe monitoring methods for each type of supplier?
<--- Score

49. Do you expect managers to control access to information and systems?
<--- Score

50. Do you manage and control changes and enhancements to networks?
<--- Score

51. Has the improved process and its steps been standardized?
<--- Score

52. Did you think about your current information security controls?
<--- Score

53. Is there a standardized process?
<--- Score

54. Who has control over resources?
<--- Score

55. Do you describe how you plan to communicate with each supplier?
<--- Score

56. How will new or emerging customer needs/requirements be checked/communicated to orient the process toward meeting the new specifications and continually reducing variation?
<--- Score

57. Do you monitor how critical suppliers respond to incidents?

<--- Score

58. Do you create information accuracy and completeness controls?

<--- Score

59. Do you manage and control changes in suppliers and contractors?

<--- Score

60. Is reporting being used or needed?

<--- Score

61. How will the process owner and team be able to hold the gains?

<--- Score

62. Does a troubleshooting guide exist or is it needed?

<--- Score

63. Do you teach people about your information security controls?

<--- Score

64. Are pertinent alerts monitored, analyzed and distributed to appropriate personnel?

<--- Score

65. Do you describe rules to control the use of subcontractors by suppliers?

<--- Score

66. Do you support monitoring by providing needed skills and resources?

<--- Score

67. What key inputs and outputs are being measured on an ongoing basis?
<--- Score

68. What are your results for key measures or indicators of the accomplishment of your ISO IEC 27002 strategy and action plans, including building and strengthening core competencies?
<--- Score

69. In the 27000 standards family, what is the function of ISO/IEC 27002?
<--- Score

70. Did you establish a policy to control supplier access to your information?
<--- Score

71. How will the process owner verify improvement in present and future sigma levels, process capabilities?
<--- Score

72. Do you make sure that background verifications comply with all relevant laws and regulations and with all relevant ethical standards?
<--- Score

73. Do you control how suppliers protect sensitive information?
<--- Score

74. Do you manage and control the use of new technologies and techniques?

<--- Score

75. Do you monitor compliance with information security requirements?
<--- Score

76. Is there an action plan in case of emergencies?
<--- Score

77. How do you monitor usage and cost?
<--- Score

78. Did you describe specific access controls for each type of supplier?
<--- Score

79. Do you describe the controls that each party must implement?
<--- Score

80. What is your theory of human motivation, and how does your compensation plan fit with that view?
<--- Score

81. Do you retain control over how suppliers manage security?
<--- Score

82. What is the recommended frequency of auditing?
<--- Score

83. What other systems, operations, processes, and infrastructures (hiring practices, staffing, training, incentives/rewards, metrics/dashboards/scorecards, etc.) need updates, additions, changes, or deletions in order to facilitate knowledge transfer and

improvements?
<--- Score

84. How will the day-to-day responsibilities for monitoring and continual improvement be transferred from the improvement team to the process owner?
<--- Score

85. How do you determine what to monitor?
<--- Score

86. What are you attempting to measure/monitor?
<--- Score

87. What cybersecurity standards and frameworks (if any) do you currently use?
<--- Score

88. Do you ask them to monitor critical outsourced components?
<--- Score

89. Do you manage and control how security incidents are resolved?
<--- Score

90. Or nist as the standard of measurement?
<--- Score

91. Do you manage and control the use of new products and new versions?
<--- Score

92. Will any special training be provided for results interpretation?

<--- Score

93. Did you establish supplier monitoring processes and procedures?

<--- Score

94. Do you describe controls suppliers must use to manage subcontractors?

<--- Score

95. Did you consider using distance learning methods?

<--- Score

96. Do you manage changes in information security controls?

<--- Score

97. Do you teach people about how others can learn more about security?

<--- Score

98. Do you teach people about how they can learn more about security?

<--- Score

99. Do you control how suppliers protect your critical facilities?

<--- Score

100. How likely is the current ISO IEC 27002 plan to come in on schedule or on budget?
<--- Score

101. What role(s) do or should national/ international standards and organizations that

develop national/ international standards play in critical infrastructure cybersecurity conformity assessment?

<--- Score

102. Is there a transfer of ownership and knowledge to process owner and process team tasked with the responsibilities.

<--- Score

103. Is there a recommended audit plan for routine surveillance inspections of ISO IEC 27002's gains?

<--- Score

104. Do you ask suppliers to report on the effectiveness of controls?

<--- Score

105. What should the next improvement project be that is related to ISO IEC 27002?

<--- Score

106. How do you establish and deploy modified action plans if circumstances require a shift in plans and rapid execution of new plans?

<--- Score

107. Did you think about your organizations information security controls?

<--- Score

108. Do you control suppliers who manage or provide critical services?

<--- Score

109. Do you describe the supplier audits that you

plan to carry out?
<--- Score

110. Do you manage and control changes in information security controls?
<--- Score

111. Do you manage and control changes in policies and procedures?
<--- Score

112. Is a response plan established and deployed?
<--- Score

113. Do you manage and control enhancements to current services?
<--- Score

114. What do you measure to verify effectiveness gains?
<--- Score

115. Is there a ISO IEC 27002 Communication plan covering who needs to get what information when?
<--- Score

116. Are documented procedures clear and easy to follow for the operators?
<--- Score

117. Do you ask suppliers to monitor critical outsourced components?
<--- Score

118. Does the response plan contain a definite closed loop continual improvement scheme (e.g., plan-do-

check-act)?

<--- Score

119. Do you describe how you plan to review the performance of suppliers?

<--- Score

120. Who is the ISO IEC 27002 process owner?

<--- Score

121. Do you retain control over how such suppliers manage security?

<--- Score

122. How do you monitor suppliers service delivery performance levels?

<--- Score

123. Do you verify that suppliers have workable service continuity plans?

<--- Score

124. Do you monitor how critical suppliers manage changes?

<--- Score

125. Do you account for why others must comply with security standards?

<--- Score

126. Do you monitor how critical suppliers identify vulnerabilities?

<--- Score

127. Do you monitor how critical suppliers report incidents?

<--- Score

128. Does job training on the documented procedures need to be part of the process team's education and training?
<--- Score

129. Are there documented procedures?
<--- Score

130. Did you specify access controls for each type of information?
<--- Score

131. Is there a control plan in place for sustaining improvements (short and long-term)?
<--- Score

132. Do you base updates on lessons learned from security incidents?
<--- Score

133. What is the control/monitoring plan?
<--- Score

Add up total points for this section:
_ _ _ _ _ = Total points for this section

Divided by: _ _ _ _ _ _ (number of statements answered) = _ _ _ _ _ _
Average score for this section

Transfer your score to the ISO IEC 27002 Index at the beginning of the Self-Assessment.

CRITERION #7: SUSTAIN:

INTENT: Retain the benefits.

In my belief, the answer to this question is clearly defined:

5 Strongly Agree

4 Agree

3 Neutral

2 Disagree

1 Strongly Disagree

1. How is siem addressed in practice?
<--- Score

2. Do you consider whether or not it is a first or repeat offence?
<--- Score

3. Who is responsible for the metrics?
<--- Score

4. Did you think about what contractors should

know about security?

<--- Score

5. Do you ensure that terms and conditions are appropriate to the job?

<--- Score

6. Do you take action whenever incidents occur and service suffers?

<--- Score

7. Do you describe the methods that may be used to provide information?

<--- Score

8. Do you schedule activities for current employees and contractors?

<--- Score

9. What relationships among ISO IEC 27002 trends do you perceive?

<--- Score

10. How is implementation research currently incorporated into each of your goals?

<--- Score

11. Who are the Sponsors?

<--- Score

12. Do you audit supplier compliance with your supplier agreements?

<--- Score

13. Do you manage the changes that you make to supplier services?

<--- Score

14. Do you ask them to ensure that critical components work as expected?
<--- Score

15. Did you clarify when background verifications should be done?
<--- Score

16. Do you provide information security briefings before granting access?
<--- Score

17. Do you describe your notification and collaboration procedures?
<--- Score

18. Do you ask them to protect the technologies that you depend upon?
<--- Score

19. Do you expect suppliers to account for incident response procedures?
<--- Score

20. Do you explain where others can get more training materials?
<--- Score

21. Do you describe how authorized persons will be assigned and removed?
<--- Score

22. Do you ask suppliers to notify you if they fail to screen personnel?

<--- Score

23. Is there a work around that you can use?
<--- Score

24. Do you make contractors aware of security responsibilities?
<--- Score

25. Do you make employees aware of security responsibilities?
<--- Score

26. Do you explain where suppliers can get more training materials?
<--- Score

27. What is the most important asset or information that is owned by your organization?
<--- Score

28. How does your organization know which services or assets to protect?
<--- Score

29. What is your competitive advantage?
<--- Score

30. Do you manage changes to supplier agreements?
<--- Score

31. Do you describe relevant information security policies for each contract?
<--- Score

32. Do you clarify information security responsibilities specific to each job?

<--- Score

33. Do you expect people to report security policy and procedure violations?

<--- Score

34. If you find that you havent accomplished one of the goals for one of the steps of the ISO IEC 27002 strategy, what will you do to fix it?

<--- Score

35. Do you describe how appropriate supplier personnel will be selected?

<--- Score

36. Do you provide information security guidelines before granting access?

<--- Score

37. Do you manage changes in information security procedures?

<--- Score

38. Did you clarify who is allowed to do background verifications?

<--- Score

39. Did you think about what your awareness program should consider?

<--- Score

40. Do you account for why suppliers must comply with security legislation?

<--- Score

41. Do you ask them to share information about component lifecycles?
<--- Score

42. At what moment would you think; Will I get fired?
<--- Score

43. Did you consider using campaigns to raise security awareness?
<--- Score

44. Did you think about the jobs people do and what you expect from them?
<--- Score

45. Do you do more checks if candidates will handle confidential information?
<--- Score

46. Do you teach people about the information that must be protected?
<--- Score

47. Did you consider scheduling regular security awareness activities?
<--- Score

48. Do you account for why others must comply with rules and regulations?
<--- Score

49. Do you clarify information security roles and responsibilities?
<--- Score

50. Do you expect managers to motivate employees and contractors?
<--- Score

51. Do you account for why personal accountability is so important?
<--- Score

52. Do you use contractual terms and conditions to specify your employees information security responsibilities?
<--- Score

53. Do you explain who others can contact to get more information?
<--- Score

54. Can support from partners be adjusted?
<--- Score

55. Do you expect managers to enforce security policies and procedures?
<--- Score

56. Do you use agreements to ensure that screening takes place?
<--- Score

57. Are corresponding practices widely used throughout critical infrastructure and industry?
<--- Score

58. Did you think about what kinds of information should be protected?
<--- Score

59. What you have to protect ?
<--- Score

60. Do you make sure that a breach has occurred before you take action?
<--- Score

61. Do you clarify how information will be moved safely and securely?
<--- Score

62. What is the funding source for this project?
<--- Score

63. What is the size of your security team?
<--- Score

64. Do you expect people to achieve a suitable level of security awareness?
<--- Score

65. Did you think about what employees should know about security?
<--- Score

66. Do you consider the type of information each supplier may access?
<--- Score

67. Do you describe your organizations incident management procedures?
<--- Score

68. Do you make sure that employees are aware of your security policies and procedures and are kept up-to-date with the latest changes?

<--- Score

69. Do you ask them to ensure that the origin of items can be traced?
<--- Score

70. Do you ensure that agreements are signed before access is allowed?
<--- Score

71. How do you know if your SIEM tooling and correlation rules are working correctly?
<--- Score

72. Why is it important to have senior management support for a ISO IEC 27002 project?
<--- Score

73. Do you specify contractor screening duties and responsibilities?
<--- Score

74. Do you ask suppliers to submit regular independent security reports?
<--- Score

75. Do you clarify asset protection obligations and responsibilities?
<--- Score

76. What is the estimated value of the project?
<--- Score

77. Do you consider establishing supplier authorization procedures?
<--- Score

78. Do you expect managers to provide an anonymous reporting channel?
<--- Score

79. Do you account for why others must be familiar with rules and regulations?
<--- Score

80. Do you expect suppliers to explain access authorization procedures?
<--- Score

81. Do you explain who suppliers can contact to get more information?
<--- Score

82. What are the most challenging aspects of ISO/ IEC 27002 implementation and ISO/IEC 27001 compliance?
<--- Score

83. Do you describe how and why access authorizations would be revoked?
<--- Score

84. Do you expect managers to ensure that all personnel are competent?
<--- Score

85. What ISO IEC 27002 modifications can you make work for you?
<--- Score

86. Do you safeguard information received from external parties?

<--- Score

87. Do you expect managers to enforce terms and conditions of employment?
<--- Score

88. Do you talk about relevant information security rules and regulations?
<--- Score

89. Do you consider defining supplier authorization conditions?
<--- Score

90. Do you account for why others must comply with security regulations?
<--- Score

91. Do you use contractual terms and conditions to specify your contractors information security responsibilities?
<--- Score

92. Do you account for why suppliers must comply with security policies?
<--- Score

93. Do you ask suppliers to pay special attention to critical components?
<--- Score

94. Have you established an information security awareness program?
<--- Score

95. Do you ask suppliers to tell you if items may no

longer be available?
<--- Score

96. Do you provide training before people start new jobs?
<--- Score

97. Do you account for why others must comply with security legislation?
<--- Score

98. What goals did you miss?
<--- Score

99. Do you update your information security awareness program?
<--- Score

100. Do you review information security incidents with your suppliers?
<--- Score

101. Who is going to spread your message?
<--- Score

102. Do you allocate responsibilities to both you and your suppliers?
<--- Score

103. Does the framework have significant adoption within your industry?
<--- Score

104. Do you do more detailed checks for both new hires and promotions?
<--- Score

105. Do you ask them to enforce agreements and to review compliance?

<--- Score

106. Did you consider scheduling periodic security awareness sessions?

<--- Score

107. Did you describe the information that each type of supplier may access?

<--- Score

108. Do you account for how your personnel should interact with suppliers?

<--- Score

109. What are the relationships between each tool, method and model?

<--- Score

110. Do you talk about your organizations approach to information security?

<--- Score

111. Do you clarify which information security responsibilities remain valid?

<--- Score

112. Which input sources do you use for your SIEM environment?

<--- Score

113. Do you expect suppliers to account for access authorization procedures?

<--- Score

114. Do you explain how others can access more security resources?
<--- Score

115. Did you assign responsibility for managing your supplier relationships?
<--- Score

116. Do you account for how suppliers can access more security resources?
<--- Score

117. Do you describe how and when access authorizations will be assigned?
<--- Score

118. Do you clarify security roles and responsibilities before allowing access?
<--- Score

119. What are the objectives for the ISMS?
<--- Score

120. Which of the practices pose the most significant implementation challenge?
<--- Score

121. Do you ask them to pay special attention to critical components?
<--- Score

122. Do you ensure that suppliers agree with your terms and conditions?
<--- Score

123. Who stays on top of changing regulations and security frameworks?

<--- Score

124. Are you / should you be revolutionary or evolutionary?

<--- Score

125. Do you ask suppliers to protect the technologies that you depend upon?

<--- Score

126. Do you clarify the access that suppliers may be allowed to have?

<--- Score

127. Do you tell job candidates that they will be expected to sign agreements?

<--- Score

128. Do you ask both employees and contractors to sign agreements?

<--- Score

129. Do you clarify suppliers information security duties and obligations?

<--- Score

130. Do you determine the suitability of all information security candidates?

<--- Score

131. Do you clarify what must be done when screening is not completed?

<--- Score

132. Do you ask suppliers to notify you if others fail to screen personnel?
<--- Score

133. Did you consider using booklets and newsletters to raise awareness?
<--- Score

134. Do you review the information security aspects of each relationship?
<--- Score

135. Do you draft confidentiality and nondisclosure agreements?
<--- Score

136. Do you review how well security incidents are being handled?
<--- Score

137. Do you establish joint resilience and recovery arrangements?
<--- Score

138. Do you check the candidates financial credit history?
<--- Score

139. Do you expect all personnel to use the appropriate work methods?
<--- Score

140. Did you think about how your awareness program should be delivered?
<--- Score

141. Do you account for why others must comply with security agreements?

<--- Score

142. Are you maintaining a past–present–future perspective throughout the ISO IEC 27002 discussion?

<--- Score

143. Do you teach people about your information security procedures?

<--- Score

144. Are all business units included in the ISMS?

<--- Score

145. Is ISO IEC 27002 dependent on the successful delivery of a current project?

<--- Score

146. Do you clarify how other peoples information must be handled?

<--- Score

147. Do you use contractual terms and conditions to specify your organizations information security responsibilities?

<--- Score

148. Do you teach people about your clear desk and screen policy?

<--- Score

149. How will you motivate the stakeholders with the least vested interest?

<--- Score

150. Do you audit supplier service delivery and information security?

<--- Score

151. Do you ask suppliers to assign someone to manage service agreements?

<--- Score

152. Is information security seen as important within your organization?

<--- Score

153. What additional approaches already exist?

<--- Score

154. What is the craziest thing you can do?

<--- Score

155. Do you account for where suppliers can get more training materials?

<--- Score

156. Do you consider privacy legislation when verifications are done?

<--- Score

157. Do you ask suppliers to ensure that critical components work as expected?

<--- Score

158. How will you insure seamless interoperability of ISO IEC 27002 moving forward?

<--- Score

159. Does your organization implement forced password changes?

<--- Score

160. Do you clarify all relevant legal obligations and responsibilities?
<--- Score

161. Do you check the candidates personal identity?
<--- Score

162. Do you check the personal history of all candidates?
<--- Score

163. Do you explain why suppliers must comply with security policies?
<--- Score

164. Do you clarify which legal responsibilities remain valid after termination?
<--- Score

165. Do you make it clear that security violations will not be tolerated?
<--- Score

166. Do you expect them to validate technology products and services?
<--- Score

167. Do you use your awareness program to talk about information security?
<--- Score

168. To whom or what department do you report?
<--- Score

169. What role does communication play in the success or failure of a ISO IEC 27002 project?
<--- Score

170. Do you account for who suppliers can contact to get more information?
<--- Score

171. Why adopt a framework?
<--- Score

172. If you do not follow, then how to lead?
<--- Score

173. Do you ask them to protect it and communication technologies?
<--- Score

174. Do you account for how contractors can meet responsibilities?
<--- Score

175. Do you ask suppliers to share information about component lifecycles?
<--- Score

176. Do you establish notification procedures that screeners must use?
<--- Score

177. Do you schedule activities for people with new roles or positions?
<--- Score

178. Do you expect them to share information

about supply chains?

<--- Score

179. Do you expect suppliers to share information about supply chains?

<--- Score

180. Do you check to see if candidate has a criminal record?

<--- Score

181. The political context: who holds power?

<--- Score

182. Do you review service delivery reports generated by your suppliers?

<--- Score

183. Do you prepare information security agreements for each supplier?

<--- Score

184. Do you review the relationship suppliers have with own suppliers?

<--- Score

185. Do you clarify your suppliers resilience and recovery obligations?

<--- Score

186. How do you create buy-in?

<--- Score

187. Do you review supplier compliance with your supplier agreements?

<--- Score

188. Do you review the information security aspects of this relationship?
<--- Score

189. Do you ensure that others agree with your terms and conditions?
<--- Score

190. Do you make sure that your organizations employees receive regular information security briefings and updates?
<--- Score

191. Do you perform more rigorous background checks on people who will be handling sensitive information?
<--- Score

192. Do you clarify information security obligations and responsibilities?
<--- Score

193. Do you account for why others must comply with security contracts?
<--- Score

194. Do you expect managers to act as information security role models?
<--- Score

195. Who are the key stakeholders?
<--- Score

196. Did you ensure that the program complies with your security procedures?

<--- Score

197. Do you ensure that agreements comply with your security policies?
<--- Score

198. Do you tell job candidates that others will be expected to sign agreements?
<--- Score

199. Do you ask suppliers to ensure that the origin of items can be traced?
<--- Score

200. Did you think about your organizations specific security obligations?
<--- Score

201. Do others ensure that people continue to have the right knowledge?
<--- Score

202. Do you ensure that information services are properly protected?
<--- Score

203. Do you see if it still complies with security policies and procedures?
<--- Score

204. How do you transition from the baseline to the target?
<--- Score

205. Do you describe suppliers reporting obligations and responsibilities?

<--- Score

206. Do you ask suppliers to protect IT and communication technologies?
<--- Score

207. Do you ask them to safeguard the services that others subcontract?
<--- Score

208. Do you review the relationship suppliers have with their own suppliers?
<--- Score

209. Did you clarify why background verifications are important?
<--- Score

210. Do you assign responsibility for handling information security incidents?
<--- Score

211. How do you keep the momentum going?
<--- Score

212. When did you start implementing your SIEM environment and/or tooling?
<--- Score

213. Do you check the candidates character references?
<--- Score

214. Do you consider how much security training the offender has?
<--- Score

215. Do you ask suppliers to implement security throughout supply chains?
<--- Score

216. Do you account for how employees can meet responsibilities?
<--- Score

217. Do you consider the nature and the gravity of security breaches?
<--- Score

218. Do you describe the information classification scheme that will be used?
<--- Score

219. Do you account for whose information must be protected and why?
<--- Score

220. Do you frequently assess if IT still complies with security policies and procedures?
<--- Score

221. Do you clarify information security responsibilities when job duties change?
<--- Score

222. Who is on the team?
<--- Score

223. Do you manage changes to services provided by suppliers?
<--- Score

224. Do you account for how people will work together if incidents occur?

<--- Score

225. Have you established information security agreements with each supplier?

<--- Score

226. Do you teach people about your incident reporting procedures?

<--- Score

227. Do you ask them to safeguard the components that others buy?

<--- Score

228. Do you respect all relevant legislation when you do background checks?

<--- Score

229. Locations or facilities covered by the ISMS; are there any logical boundaries?

<--- Score

230. Do you safeguard information received from other companies?

<--- Score

231. Do you consider whether or not it is a deliberate breach?

<--- Score

232. Do you make sure that your organizations contractors receive regular information security briefings and updates?

<--- Score

233. Do you describe the methods that may be used to access information?

<--- Score

234. Do you make sure that contractors are aware of your security policies and procedures and are kept up-to-date with the latest changes?

<--- Score

235. Do you describe the type of information that may be provided or accessed?

<--- Score

236. Do you explain how suppliers can access more security resources?

<--- Score

237. Do you check candidates character references?

<--- Score

238. Do you check compliance with information security agreements?

<--- Score

239. Do you review supplier service delivery and information security?

<--- Score

240. Did you ensure that the program complies with your security policies?

<--- Score

241. Do you clarify the actions and legal steps that will be taken?

<--- Score

242. Do you explain why others must comply with security policies?
<--- Score

243. Do you account for that obligations may continue after job ends?
<--- Score

244. Who do we want your customers to become?
<--- Score

245. Do you study reports produced by independent auditors (if available)?
<--- Score

246. Do you use contractual agreements to protect confidential information?
<--- Score

247. Do you prepare suitable confidentiality and nondisclosure agreements?
<--- Score

248. Have you established personnel background verification procedures?
<--- Score

249. Do you ask them to tell you if items may no longer be available?
<--- Score

250. Do you distinguish between types of suppliers and types of access?
<--- Score

251. Do you expect managers to make people aware of responsibilities?

<--- Score

252. How do you use threat intelligence with your SIEM?

<--- Score

253. Who is concerned about information security?

<--- Score

254. In a project to restructure ISO IEC 27002 outcomes, which stakeholders would you involve?

<--- Score

255. Did you consider using department-based teaching methods?

<--- Score

256. Do you ask suppliers to enforce agreements and to review compliance?

<--- Score

257. Do you consider creating explicit lists of authorized personnel?

<--- Score

258. Do you manage the changes that suppliers make to services?

<--- Score

259. Do you talk about your organizations information security expectations?

<--- Score

260. Do you ensure that information is appropriately classified?
<--- Score

261. How do you ensure that implementations of ISO IEC 27002 products are done in a way that ensures safety?
<--- Score

262. Did you think about how awareness activities should be scheduled?
<--- Score

263. Did you assign this job to an individual or service management team?
<--- Score

264. Did you establish an awareness program to talk about supplier security?
<--- Score

265. Do you consider employment legislation when verifications are done?
<--- Score

266. Do you schedule activities for new employees and contractors?
<--- Score

267. Do you describe acceptable and unacceptable uses of information?
<--- Score

268. Do you consider managements commitment to information security?
<--- Score

269. What is the structure of your IT security organization?

<--- Score

270. Do you account for who ise information must be protected and why?

<--- Score

271. What unique value proposition (UVP) do you offer?

<--- Score

272. What safeguards are available?

<--- Score

273. Do you manage changes in information security policies?

<--- Score

274. Do you check the backgrounds of all candidates for employment?

<--- Score

275. Do you prepare supply chain security agreements with your suppliers?

<--- Score

276. Do you teach people about information security responsibilities?

<--- Score

Add up total points for this section:
_ _ _ _ _ = Total points for this section

Divided by: _ _ _ _ _ _ (number of

statements answered) = _ _ _ _ _ _
Average score for this section

Transfer your score to the ISO IEC 27002
Index at the beginning of the Self-
Assessment.

ISO IEC 27002 and Managing Projects, Criteria for Project Managers:

1.0 Initiating Process Group: ISO IEC 27002

1. How well did the chosen processes produce the expected results?

2. Who is involved in each phase?

3. How well did the chosen processes fit the needs of the ISO IEC 27002 project?

4. What will be the pressing issues of tomorrow?

5. Although the ISO IEC 27002 project manager does not directly manage procurement and contracting activities, who does manage procurement and contracting activities in your organization then if not the PM?

6. Which of six sigmas dmaic phases focuses on the measurement of internal process that affect factors that are critical to quality?

7. Where must it be done?

8. Are identified risks being monitored properly, are new risks arising during the ISO IEC 27002 project or are foreseen risks occurring?

9. Do you know all the stakeholders impacted by the ISO IEC 27002 project and what needs are?

10. How will you know you did it?

11. Who supports, improves, and oversees

standardized processes related to the ISO IEC 27002 projects program?

12. The ISO IEC 27002 project you are managing has nine stakeholders. How many channel of communications are there between corresponding stakeholders?

13. What are the tools and techniques to be used in each phase?

14. What were things that you did very well and want to do the same again on the next ISO IEC 27002 project?

15. If action is called for, what form should it take?

16. Did the ISO IEC 27002 project team have the right skills?

17. Have requirements been tested, approved, and fulfill the ISO IEC 27002 project scope?

18. Were decisions made in a timely manner?

19. What areas does the group agree are the biggest success on the ISO IEC 27002 project?

20. What will you do?

1.1 Project Charter: ISO IEC 27002

21. What ideas do you have for initial tests of change (PDSA cycles)?

22. Success determination factors: how will the success of the ISO IEC 27002 project be determined from the customers perspective?

23. What are the constraints?

24. How will you know a change is an improvement?

25. Major high-level milestone targets: what events measure progress?

26. Who ise input and support will this ISO IEC 27002 project require?

27. What is the most common tool for helping define the detail?

28. Assumptions and constraints: what assumptions were made in defining the ISO IEC 27002 project?

29. Where does all this information come from?

30. Market – identify products market, including whether it is outside of the objective: what is the purpose of the program or ISO IEC 27002 project?

31. What are the deliverables?

32. ISO IEC 27002 project background: what is the

primary motivation for this ISO IEC 27002 project?

33. When will this occur?

34. Must Have?

35. Will this replace an existing product?

36. Why executive support?

37. Run it as as a startup?

38. What are the assumptions?

39. How much?

40. How will you learn more about the process or system you are trying to improve?

1.2 Stakeholder Register: ISO IEC 27002

41. What is the power of the stakeholder?

42. Who are the stakeholders?

43. Who is managing stakeholder engagement?

44. How will reports be created?

45. What are the major ISO IEC 27002 project milestones requiring communications or providing communications opportunities?

46. What opportunities exist to provide communications?

47. How much influence do they have on the ISO IEC 27002 project?

48. Is your organization ready for change?

49. How should employers make voices heard?

50. How big is the gap?

51. What & Why?

52. Who wants to talk about Security?

1.3 Stakeholder Analysis Matrix: ISO IEC 27002

53. How will the ISO IEC 27002 project benefit them?

54. Are the required specifications for products or services changing?

55. Do the stakeholders goals and expectations support or conflict with the ISO IEC 27002 project goals?

56. What do you need to appraise?

57. Who will be affected by the ISO IEC 27002 project?

58. New technologies, services, ideas?

59. Sustainable financial backing?

60. How affected by the problem(s)?

61. Economy - home, abroad?

62. Legislative effects?

63. Who is influential in the ISO IEC 27002 project area (both thematic and geographic areas)?

64. Disadvantages of proposition?

65. Are there different rules or organizational models for men and women?

66. Business and product development?

67. Identify the stakeholders levels most frequently used –or at least sought– in your ISO IEC 27002 projects and for which purpose?

68. Usps (unique selling points)?

69. Market developments?

70. Location and geographical?

71. What is your Advocacy Strategy?

2.0 Planning Process Group: ISO IEC 27002

72. To what extent is the program helping to influence your organizations policy framework?

73. The ISO IEC 27002 project charter is created in which ISO IEC 27002 project management process group?

74. How many days can task X be late in starting without affecting the ISO IEC 27002 project completion date?

75. In what way has the program contributed towards the issue culture and development included on the public agenda?

76. Is the pace of implementing the products of the program ensuring the completeness of the results of the ISO IEC 27002 project?

77. What are the different approaches to building the WBS?

78. What factors are contributing to progress or delay in the achievement of products and results?

79. Is the identification of the problems, inequalities and gaps, with respective causes, clear in the ISO IEC 27002 project?

80. Why is it important to determine activity

sequencing on ISO IEC 27002 projects?

81. Who are the ISO IEC 27002 project stakeholders?

82. In which ISO IEC 27002 project management process group is the detailed ISO IEC 27002 project budget created?

83. What input will you be required to provide the ISO IEC 27002 project team?

84. Are the necessary foundations in place to ensure the sustainability of the results of the ISO IEC 27002 project?

85. What do you need to do?

86. To what extent have the target population and participants made the activities own, taking an active role in it?

87. How well will the chosen processes produce the expected results?

88. Do the partners have sufficient financial capacity to keep up the benefits produced by the programme?

89. Have operating capacities been created and/or reinforced in partners?

90. To what extent are the visions and actions of the partners consistent or divergent with regard to the program?

91. Will you be replaced?

2.1 Project Management Plan: ISO IEC 27002

92. Are cost risk analysis methods applied to develop contingencies for the estimated total ISO IEC 27002 project costs?

93. Is the budget realistic?

94. What if, for example, the positive direction and vision of your organization causes expected trends to change resulting in greater need than expected?

95. Are there any client staffing expectations?

96. What does management expect of PMs?

97. Are calculations and results of analyzes essentially correct?

98. What did not work so well?

99. If the ISO IEC 27002 project is complex or scope is specialized, do you have appropriate and/or qualified staff available to perform the tasks?

100. Did the planning effort collaborate to develop solutions that integrate expertise, policies, programs, and ISO IEC 27002 projects across entities?

101. What data/reports/tools/etc. do your PMs need?

102. What is ISO IEC 27002 project scope

management?

103. Is mitigation authorized or recommended?

104. Who is the sponsor?

105. How do you organize the costs in the ISO IEC 27002 project management plan?

106. Does the implementation plan have an appropriate division of responsibilities?

107. When is the ISO IEC 27002 project management plan created?

108. What is the business need?

109. Are there non-structural buyout or relocation recommendations?

110. Do there need to be organizational changes?

2.2 Scope Management Plan: ISO IEC 27002

111. Is documentation created for communication with the suppliers and Vendors?

112. Have the key elements of a coherent ISO IEC 27002 project management strategy been established?

113. Has the schedule been baselined?

114. Have all unresolved risks been documented?

115. Is there an issues management plan in place?

116. Are tasks tracked by hours?

117. Have adequate resources been provided by management to ensure ISO IEC 27002 project success?

118. What are the risks that could significantly affect procuring consultant staff for the ISO IEC 27002 project?

119. Are ISO IEC 27002 project team members committed fulltime?

120. Process groups – where do scope management processes fit in?

121. Are ISO IEC 27002 project leaders committed to

this ISO IEC 27002 project full time?

122. Assess the expected stability of the scope of this ISO IEC 27002 project how likely is it to change, how frequently, and by how much?

123. What strengths do you have?

124. Are decisions captured in a decisions log?

125. Has the ISO IEC 27002 project manager been identified?

126. Timeline and milestones?

127. Is there a formal set of procedures supporting Stakeholder Management?

128. Are internal ISO IEC 27002 project status meetings held at reasonable intervals?

129. How are you planning to maintain the scope baseline and how will you manage scope changes?

130. Has a resource management plan been created?

2.3 Requirements Management Plan: ISO IEC 27002

131. Is infrastructure setup part of your ISO IEC 27002 project?

132. What are you trying to do?

133. Will you document changes to requirements?

134. Did you provide clear and concise specifications?

135. Has the requirements team been instructed in the Change Control process?

136. Is there formal agreement on who has authority to approve a change in requirements?

137. Is there formal agreement on who has authority to request a change in requirements?

138. What is a problem?

139. If it exists, where is it housed?

140. What performance metrics will be used?

141. Do you understand the role that each stakeholder will play in the requirements process?

142. Who is responsible for quantifying the ISO IEC 27002 project requirements?

143. Who came up with this requirement?

144. Does the ISO IEC 27002 project have a Change Control process?

145. What went right?

146. How will bidders price evaluations be done, by deliverables, phases, or in a big bang?

147. When and how will a requirements baseline be established in this ISO IEC 27002 project?

148. Subject to change control?

149. Are actual resource expenditures versus planned still acceptable?

150. Is stakeholder risk tolerance an important factor for the requirements process in this ISO IEC 27002 project?

2.4 Requirements Documentation: ISO IEC 27002

151. Where do you define what is a customer, what are the attributes of customer?

152. How can you document system requirements?

153. What variations exist for a process?

154. What happens when requirements are wrong?

155. How do you get the user to tell you what they want?

156. How to document system requirements?

157. What are the potential disadvantages/ advantages?

158. Can the requirements be checked?

159. Are all functions required by the customer included?

160. Does the system provide the functions which best support the customers needs?

161. What images does it conjure?

162. Are there any requirements conflicts?

163. Basic work/business process; high-level, what is

being touched?

164. What are current process problems?

165. Is the requirement properly understood?

166. What if the system wasn t implemented?

167. Have the benefits identified with the system being identified clearly?

168. How does what is being described meet the business need?

169. Validity. does the system provide the functions which best support the customers needs?

170. Where are business rules being captured?

2.5 Requirements Traceability Matrix: ISO IEC 27002

171. How small is small enough?

172. Describe the process for approving requirements so they can be added to the traceability matrix and ISO IEC 27002 project work can be performed. Will the ISO IEC 27002 project requirements become approved in writing?

173. What are the chronologies, contingencies, consequences, criteria?

174. Why do you manage scope?

175. How do you manage scope?

176. Is there a requirements traceability process in place?

177. Will you use a Requirements Traceability Matrix?

178. Do you have a clear understanding of all subcontracts in place?

179. Why use a WBS?

180. What percentage of ISO IEC 27002 projects are producing traceability matrices between requirements and other work products?

181. How will it affect the stakeholders personally in

career?

182. What is the WBS?

2.6 Project Scope Statement: ISO IEC 27002

183. Is this process communicated to the customer and team members?

184. Are there specific processes you will use to evaluate and approve/reject changes?

185. Will the ISO IEC 27002 project risks be managed according to the ISO IEC 27002 projects risk management process?

186. Elements of scope management that deal with concept development ?

187. Will all tasks resulting from issues be entered into the ISO IEC 27002 project Plan and tracked through the plan?

188. Is the plan for your organization of the ISO IEC 27002 project resources adequate?

189. Will this process be communicated to the customer and ISO IEC 27002 project team?

190. Risks?

191. Has everyone approved the ISO IEC 27002 projects scope statement?

192. Are there backup strategies for key members of the ISO IEC 27002 project?

193. What are the major deliverables of the ISO IEC 27002 project?

194. Have you been able to thoroughly document the ISO IEC 27002 projects assumptions and constraints?

195. Is there a process (test plans, inspections, reviews) defined for verifying outputs for each task?

196. Why do you need to manage scope?

197. Elements that deal with providing the detail?

198. Do you anticipate new stakeholders joining the ISO IEC 27002 project over time?

199. What should you drop in order to add something new?

2.7 Assumption and Constraint Log: ISO IEC 27002

200. If appropriate, is the deliverable content consistent with current ISO IEC 27002 project documents and in compliance with the Document Management Plan?

201. Have adequate resources been provided by management to ensure ISO IEC 27002 project success?

202. Is the amount of effort justified by the anticipated value of forming a new process?

203. Can the requirements be traced to the appropriate components of the solution, as well as test scripts?

204. Diagrams and tables are included to account for complex concepts and increase overall readability?

205. Are there nonconformance issues?

206. Does the ISO IEC 27002 project have a formal ISO IEC 27002 project Plan?

207. Are requirements management tracking tools and procedures in place?

208. Is the steering committee active in ISO IEC 27002 project oversight?

209. Are funding and staffing resource estimates sufficiently detailed and documented for use in planning and tracking the ISO IEC 27002 project?

210. Are there processes in place to ensure internal consistency between the source code components?

211. Are processes for release management of new development from coding and unit testing, to integration testing, to training, and production defined and followed?

212. Has a ISO IEC 27002 project Communications Plan been developed?

213. Do you know what your customers expectations are regarding this process?

214. Are formal code reviews conducted?

215. If it is out of compliance, should the process be amended or should the Plan be amended?

216. Do documented requirements exist for all critical components and areas, including technical, business, interfaces, performance, security and conversion requirements?

217. What does an audit system look like?

218. Are there processes in place to ensure that all the terms and code concepts have been documented consistently?

2.8 Work Breakdown Structure: ISO IEC 27002

219. What is the probability of completing the ISO IEC 27002 project in less that xx days?

220. Why would you develop a Work Breakdown Structure?

221. Why is it useful?

222. When do you stop?

223. What is the probability that the ISO IEC 27002 project duration will exceed xx weeks?

224. How will you and your ISO IEC 27002 project team define the ISO IEC 27002 projects scope and work breakdown structure?

225. When would you develop a Work Breakdown Structure?

226. How big is a work-package?

227. Do you need another level?

228. Can you make it?

229. Who has to do it?

230. How much detail?

231. How far down?

232. Where does it take place?

233. When does it have to be done?

234. Is the work breakdown structure (wbs) defined and is the scope of the ISO IEC 27002 project clear with assigned deliverable owners?

235. Is it a change in scope?

236. Is it still viable?

237. What has to be done?

2.9 WBS Dictionary: ISO IEC 27002

238. Are indirect costs accumulated for comparison with the corresponding budgets?

239. Authorization to proceed with all authorized work?

240. Are direct or indirect cost adjustments being accomplished according to accounting procedures acceptable to us?

241. Are detailed work packages planned as far in advance as practicable?

242. The wbs is developed as part of a joint planning session. and how do you know that youhave done this right?

243. Detailed schedules which support control account and work package start and completion dates/events?

244. Does the contractor have procedures which permit identification of recurring or non-recurring costs as necessary?

245. Are the contractors estimates of costs at completion reconcilable with cost data reported to us?

246. The anticipated business volume?

247. Are budgets or values assigned to work packages

and planning packages in terms of dollars, hours, or other measurable units?

248. Are the bases and rates for allocating costs from each indirect pool to commercial work consistent with the already stated used to allocate corresponding costs to Government contracts?

249. Are the responsibilities and authorities of each of the above organizational elements or managers clearly defined?

250. Are work packages reasonably short in time duration or do they have adequate objective indicators/milestones to minimize subjectivity of the in process work evaluation?

251. Does the contractors system include procedures for measuring the performance of critical subcontractors?

252. Major functional areas of contract effort?

253. Changes in the nature of the overhead requirements?

254. Are retroactive changes to BCWS and BCWP prohibited except for correction of errors or for normal accounting adjustments?

255. Are data elements summarized through the functional organizational structure for progressively higher levels of management?

2.10 Schedule Management Plan: ISO IEC 27002

256. Can additional resources be added to subsequent tasks to reduce the durations of the already stated tasks?

257. Have the key functions and capabilities been defined and assigned to each release or iteration?

258. Are the constraints or deadlines associated with the task accurate?

259. Is there a set of procedures defining the scope, procedures, and deliverables defining quality control?

260. Are the appropriate IT resources adequate to meet planned commitments?

261. Are the activity durations realistic and at an appropriate level of detail for effective management?

262. Are all activities captured and do they address all approved work scope in the ISO IEC 27002 project baseline?

263. What weaknesses do you have?

264. Are written status reports provided on a designated frequent basis?

265. Time for overtime?

266. Are meeting objectives identified for each meeting?

267. Does the time ISO IEC 27002 projection include an amount for contingencies (time reserves)?

268. Were ISO IEC 27002 project team members involved in detailed estimating and scheduling?

269. Are risk triggers captured?

270. Must the ISO IEC 27002 project be complete by a specified date?

271. Does the schedule have reasonable float?

272. Are the schedule estimates reasonable given the ISO IEC 27002 project?

273. Are all activities logically sequenced?

274. Are assumptions being identified, recorded, analyzed, qualified and closed?

2.11 Activity List: ISO IEC 27002

275. Where will it be performed?

276. What is the total time required to complete the ISO IEC 27002 project if no delays occur?

277. Should you include sub-activities?

278. What is the probability the ISO IEC 27002 project can be completed in xx weeks?

279. How much slack is available in the ISO IEC 27002 project?

280. What is your organizations history in doing similar activities?

281. Is infrastructure setup part of your ISO IEC 27002 project?

282. What is the LF and LS for each activity?

283. What are you counting on?

284. For other activities, how much delay can be tolerated?

285. Are the required resources available or need to be acquired?

286. What are the critical bottleneck activities?

287. How detailed should a ISO IEC 27002 project get?

288. What went well?

289. What will be performed?

290. What went wrong?

291. Is there anything planned that does not need to be here?

292. How can the ISO IEC 27002 project be displayed graphically to better visualize the activities?

293. In what sequence?

2.12 Activity Attributes: ISO IEC 27002

294. Would you consider either of corresponding activities an outlier?

295. Where else does it apply?

296. What is missing?

297. How else could the items be grouped?

298. What activity do you think you should spend the most time on?

299. Which method produces the more accurate cost assignment?

300. Have constraints been applied to the start and finish milestones for the phases?

301. Why?

302. Is there a trend during the year?

303. Can more resources be added?

304. Are the required resources available?

305. Activity: what is Missing?

306. How do you manage time?

307. Were there other ways you could have organized the data to achieve similar results?

308. How difficult will it be to do specific activities on this ISO IEC 27002 project?

309. Activity: fair or not fair?

2.13 Milestone List: ISO IEC 27002

310. Gaps in capabilities?

311. Level of the Innovation?

312. How late can each activity be finished and started?

313. Information and research?

314. How soon can the activity start?

315. Insurmountable weaknesses?

316. How will the milestone be verified?

317. Sustaining internal capabilities?

318. How will you get the word out to customers?

319. What are your competitors vulnerabilities?

320. How difficult will it be to do specific activities on this ISO IEC 27002 project?

321. Loss of key staff?

322. How late can the activity finish?

323. Environmental effects?

324. What date will the task finish?

325. Reliability of data, plan predictability?

2.14 Network Diagram: ISO IEC 27002

326. How difficult will it be to do specific activities on this ISO IEC 27002 project?

327. If a current contract exists, can you provide the vendor name, contract start, and contract expiration date?

328. Planning: who, how long, what to do?

329. What are the tools?

330. What job or jobs follow it?

331. What activity must be completed immediately before this activity can start?

332. Where do you schedule uncertainty time?

333. Are you on time?

334. Where do schedules come from?

335. If x is long, what would be the completion time if you break x into two parallel parts of y weeks and z weeks?

336. What must be completed before an activity can be started?

337. What job or jobs could run concurrently?

338. How confident can you be in your milestone

dates and the delivery date?

339. What activities must follow this activity?

340. If the ISO IEC 27002 project network diagram cannot change and you have extra personnel resources, what is the BEST thing to do?

341. Are the gantt chart and/or network diagram updated periodically and used to assess the overall ISO IEC 27002 project timetable?

342. Review the logical flow of the network diagram. Take a look at which activities you have first and then sequence the activities. Do they make sense?

343. What is the completion time?

344. Why must you schedule milestones, such as reviews, throughout the ISO IEC 27002 project?

2.15 Activity Resource Requirements: ISO IEC 27002

345. Do you use tools like decomposition and rolling-wave planning to produce the activity list and other outputs?

346. Are there unresolved issues that need to be addressed?

347. How many signatures do you require on a check and does this match what is in your policy and procedures?

348. What is the Work Plan Standard?

349. Why do you do that?

350. Anything else?

351. What are constraints that you might find during the Human Resource Planning process?

352. Organizational Applicability?

353. Other support in specific areas?

354. Which logical relationship does the PDM use most often?

355. How do you handle petty cash?

356. When does monitoring begin?

2.16 Resource Breakdown Structure: ISO IEC 27002

357. Who is allowed to perform which functions?

358. How difficult will it be to do specific activities on this ISO IEC 27002 project?

359. What is the purpose of assigning and documenting responsibility?

360. The list could probably go on, but, the thing that you would most like to know is, How long & How much?

361. Who needs what information?

362. Goals for the ISO IEC 27002 project. What is each stakeholders desired outcome for the ISO IEC 27002 project?

363. What is the number one predictor of a groups productivity?

364. What are the requirements for resource data?

365. Why is this important?

366. Who delivers the information?

367. How can this help you with team building?

368. When do they need the information?

369. Who will be used as a ISO IEC 27002 project team member?

370. Is predictive resource analysis being done?

371. Which resource planning tool provides information on resource responsibility and accountability?

372. Changes based on input from stakeholders?

373. What is each stakeholders desired outcome for the ISO IEC 27002 project?

2.17 Activity Duration Estimates: ISO IEC 27002

374. Which does one need in order to complete schedule development?

375. Why time management?

376. Who will provide training for the new application?

377. What are the three main outputs of quality control?

378. Are steps identified by which ISO IEC 27002 project documents may be changed?

379. Calculate the expected duration for an activity that has a most likely time of 3, a pessimistic time of 10, and a optimiztic time of 2?

380. Are ISO IEC 27002 project costs tracked in the general ledger?

381. What is the critical path for this ISO IEC 27002 project and how long is it?

382. Is the work performed reviewed against contractual objectives?

383. Explanation notice how many choices are half right?

384. ISO IEC 27002 project has three critical paths. Which BEST describes how this affects the ISO IEC 27002 project?

385. Find an example of a contract for information technology services. Analyze the key features of the contract. What type of contract was used and why?

386. Are team building activities completed to improve team performance?

387. Are reward and recognition systems defined to promote or reinforce desired behavior?

388. Is the cost performance monitored to identify variances from the plan?

389. Are measurement techniques employed to determine the potential impact of proposed changes?

390. What are the advantages and disadvantages of PERT?

391. Briefly summarize the work done by Maslow, Herzberg, McClellan, McGregor, Ouchi, Thamhain and Wilemon, and Covey. How do theories relate to ISO IEC 27002 project management?

392. What are the key components of a ISO IEC 27002 project communications plan?

393. What are the ways to create and distribute ISO IEC 27002 project performance information?

2.18 Duration Estimating Worksheet: ISO IEC 27002

394. Why estimate costs?

395. Is the ISO IEC 27002 project responsive to community need?

396. Will the ISO IEC 27002 project collaborate with the local community and leverage resources?

397. Is a construction detail attached (to aid in explanation)?

398. What work will be included in the ISO IEC 27002 project?

399. What is your role?

400. Define the work as completely as possible. What work will be included in the ISO IEC 27002 project?

401. Science = process: remember the scientific method?

402. Why estimate time and cost?

403. Is this operation cost effective?

404. Value pocket identification & quantification what are value pockets?

405. Small or large ISO IEC 27002 project?

406. What is the total time required to complete the ISO IEC 27002 project if no delays occur?

407. When, then?

408. When do the individual activities need to start and finish?

409. Can the ISO IEC 27002 project be constructed as planned?

2.19 Project Schedule: ISO IEC 27002

410. Did the ISO IEC 27002 project come in on schedule?

411. What does that mean?

412. Are procedures defined by which the ISO IEC 27002 project schedule may be changed?

413. Are all remaining durations correct?

414. Are there activities that came from a template or previous ISO IEC 27002 project that are not applicable on this phase of this ISO IEC 27002 project?

415. How do you use schedules?

416. How can you minimize or control changes to ISO IEC 27002 project schedules?

417. Verify that the update is accurate. Are all remaining durations correct?

418. Why is this particularly bad?

419. Meet requirements?

420. How can you fix it?

421. Have all ISO IEC 27002 project delays been adequately accounted for, communicated to all stakeholders and adjustments made in overall ISO IEC 27002 project schedule?

422. What is ISO IEC 27002 project management?

423. Why do you need to manage ISO IEC 27002 project Risk?

424. Did the ISO IEC 27002 project come in under budget?

2.20 Cost Management Plan: ISO IEC 27002

425. What would the life cycle costs be?

426. Time management – how will the schedule impact of changes be estimated and approved?

427. Published materials?

428. Are the payment terms being followed?

429. Does the ISO IEC 27002 project have a Quality Culture?

430. Vac -variance at completion, how much over/ under budget do you expect to be?

431. Best practices implementation – How will change management be applied to this ISO IEC 27002 project?

432. Are enough systems & user personnel assigned to the ISO IEC 27002 project?

433. Staffing Requirements?

434. Has the ISO IEC 27002 project scope been baselined?

435. Are schedule deliverables actually delivered?

436. Was the ISO IEC 27002 project schedule reviewed

by all stakeholders and formally accepted?

437. Exclusions – is there scope to be performed or provided by others?

438. What does this mean to a cost or scheduler manager?

439. Are metrics used to evaluate and manage Vendors?

440. Is it a ISO IEC 27002 project?

441. Is there a Steering Committee in place?

442. Are the ISO IEC 27002 project plans updated on a frequent basis?

2.21 Activity Cost Estimates: ISO IEC 27002

443. Were escalated issues resolved promptly?

444. If you are asked to lower your estimate because the price is too high, what are your options?

445. What is the ISO IEC 27002 projects sustainability strategy that will ensure ISO IEC 27002 project results will endure or be sustained?

446. Where can you get activity reports?

447. What is the activity inventory?

448. What do you want to know about the stay to know if costs were inappropriately high or low?

449. What is included in indirect cost being allocated?

450. Does the estimator have experience?

451. Performance bond should always provide what part of the contract value?

452. Were sponsors and decision makers available when needed outside regularly scheduled meetings?

453. What is procurement?

454. Who determines the quality and expertise of contractors?

455. In which phase of the acquisition process cycle does source qualifications reside?

456. What are the audit requirements?

457. How do you change activities?

458. Did the consultant work with local staff to develop local capacity?

459. What makes a good activity description?

460. Padding is bad and contingencies are good. what is the difference?

2.22 Cost Estimating Worksheet: ISO IEC 27002

461. What happens to any remaining funds not used?

462. What is the estimated labor cost today based upon this information?

463. Ask: are others positioned to know, are others credible, and will others cooperate?

464. Is it feasible to establish a control group arrangement?

465. Is the ISO IEC 27002 project responsive to community need?

466. What is the purpose of estimating?

467. Will the ISO IEC 27002 project collaborate with the local community and leverage resources?

468. What can be included?

469. How will the results be shared and to whom?

470. What additional ISO IEC 27002 project(s) could be initiated as a result of this ISO IEC 27002 project?

471. Identify the timeframe necessary to monitor progress and collect data to determine how the selected measure has changed?

472. What costs are to be estimated?

473. Does the ISO IEC 27002 project provide innovative ways for stakeholders to overcome obstacles or deliver better outcomes?

474. Can a trend be established from historical performance data on the selected measure and are the criteria for using trend analysis or forecasting methods met?

475. What info is needed?

476. Who is best positioned to know and assist in identifying corresponding factors?

477. What will others want?

2.23 Cost Baseline: ISO IEC 27002

478. Have the resources used by the ISO IEC 27002 project been reassigned to other units or ISO IEC 27002 projects?

479. Review your risk triggers -have your risks changed?

480. What is the consequence?

481. Are you meeting with your team regularly?

482. Does the suggested change request represent a desired enhancement to the products functionality?

483. Will the ISO IEC 27002 project fail if the change request is not executed?

484. Pcs for your new business. what would the life cycle costs be?

485. Have the lessons learned been filed with the ISO IEC 27002 project Management Office?

486. On budget?

487. Has the actual cost of the ISO IEC 27002 project (or ISO IEC 27002 project phase) been tallied and compared to the approved budget?

488. Has the ISO IEC 27002 project (or ISO IEC 27002 project phase) been evaluated against each objective established in the product description and Integrated

ISO IEC 27002 project Plan?

489. Have all the product or service deliverables been accepted by the customer?

490. Are you asking management for something as a result of this update?

491. Who will use corresponding metrics ?

492. How likely is it to go wrong?

493. What can go wrong?

2.24 Quality Management Plan: ISO IEC 27002

494. How many ISO IEC 27002 project staff does this specific process affect?

495. How do you ensure that protocols are up to date?

496. Are you following the quality standards?

497. Do trained quality assurance auditors conduct the audits as defined in the Quality Management Plan and scheduled by the ISO IEC 27002 project manager?

498. How is equipment calibrated?

499. What does it do for you (or to me)?

500. Checking the completeness and appropriateness of the sampling and testing. Were the right locations/ samples tested for the right parameters?

501. How are deviations from procedures handled?

502. How are changes recorded?

503. Are best practices and metrics employed to identify issues, progress, performance, etc.?

504. After observing execution of process, is it in compliance with the documented Plan?

505. How are data handled when a test is not run per

specification?

506. Have all involved stakeholders and work groups committed to the ISO IEC 27002 project?

507. Who needs a qmp?

508. Who is responsible for approving the qapp?

509. How does your organization determine the requirements and product/service features important to customers?

510. What are the appropriate test methods to be used?

511. What else should you do now?

512. What process do you use to minimize errors, defects, and rework?

513. How do you ensure that your sampling methods and procedures meet your data needs?

2.25 Quality Metrics: ISO IEC 27002

514. What is the benchmark?

515. Is there a set of procedures to capture, analyze and act on quality metrics?

516. Does risk analysis documentation meet standards?

517. What is the timeline to meet your goal?

518. Why is now the time for quality metrics?

519. Has risk analysis been adequately reviewed?

520. What happens if you get an abnormal result?

521. How is it being measured?

522. Do the operators focus on determining; is there anything you need to worry about?

523. Are there any open risk issues?

524. What documentation is required?

525. Filter visualizations of interest?

526. Who is willing to lead?

527. Have risk areas been identified?

528. What are your organizations next steps?

529. Do you stratify metrics by product or site?

530. When is the security analysis testing complete?

531. Is the reporting frequency appropriate?

532. Did the team meet the ISO IEC 27002 project success criteria documented in the Quality Metrics Matrix?

2.26 Process Improvement Plan: ISO IEC 27002

533. What actions are needed to address the problems and achieve the goals?

534. The motive is determined by asking, Why do you want to achieve this goal?

535. What personnel are the change agents for your initiative?

536. Why do you want to achieve the goal?

537. What personnel are the sponsors for that initiative?

538. To elicit goal statements, do you ask a question such as, What do you want to achieve?

539. Where do you focus?

540. What lessons have you learned so far?

541. Are you making progress on the goals?

542. Who should prepare the process improvement action plan?

543. What personnel are the champions for the initiative?

544. Management commitment at all levels?

545. What is quality and how will you ensure it?

546. What is the return on investment?

547. Have storage and access mechanisms and procedures been determined?

548. How do you measure?

549. Are you meeting the quality standards?

550. What is the test-cycle concept?

2.27 Responsibility Assignment Matrix: ISO IEC 27002

551. The total budget for the contract (including estimates for authorized and unpriced work)?

552. Are all authorized tasks assigned to identified organizational elements?

553. Are all elements of indirect expense identified to overhead cost budgets of ISO IEC 27002 projections?

554. Are estimates of costs at completion generated in a rational, consistent manner?

555. Do managers and team members provide helpful suggestions during review meetings?

556. Contract line items and end items?

557. Are the overhead pools formally and adequately identified?

558. Are the bases and rates for allocating costs from each indirect pool consistently applied?

559. Is accountability placed at the lowest-possible level within the ISO IEC 27002 project so that decisions can be made at that level?

560. What happens when others get pulled for higher priority ISO IEC 27002 projects?

561. Are others working on the right things?

562. Contemplated overhead expenditure for each period based on the best information currently available?

563. ISO IEC 27002 projected economic escalation?

564. If a role has only Signing-off, or only Communicating responsibility and has no Performing, Accountable, or Monitoring responsibility, is it necessary?

565. The staff interests – is the group or the person interested in working for this ISO IEC 27002 project?

566. Incurrence of actual indirect costs in excess of budgets, by element of expense?

567. Are overhead cost budgets established for each organization which has authority to incur overhead costs?

2.28 Roles and Responsibilities: ISO IEC 27002

568. Key conclusions and recommendations: Are conclusions and recommendations relevant and acceptable?

569. Is the data complete?

570. What expectations were met?

571. What should you do now to prepare for your career 5+ years from now?

572. What is working well within your organizations performance management system?

573. Are your budgets supportive of a culture of quality data?

574. What is working well?

575. Required skills, knowledge, experience?

576. What expectations were NOT met?

577. Is there a training program in place for stakeholders covering expectations, roles and responsibilities and any addition knowledge others need to be good stakeholders?

578. Was the expectation clearly communicated?

579. Are governance roles and responsibilities documented?

580. How is your work-life balance?

581. Who is responsible for implementation activities and where will the functions, roles and responsibilities be defined?

582. What areas of supervision are challenging for you?

583. Be specific; avoid generalities. Thank you and great work alone are insufficient. What exactly do you appreciate and why?

584. Do the values and practices inherent in the culture of your organization foster or hinder the process?

585. To decide whether to use a quality measurement, ask how will you know when it is achieved?

586. How well did the ISO IEC 27002 project Team understand the expectations of specific roles and responsibilities?

2.29 Human Resource Management Plan: ISO IEC 27002

587. Are issues raised, assessed, actioned, and resolved in a timely and efficient manner?

588. Have all involved ISO IEC 27002 project stakeholders and work groups committed to the ISO IEC 27002 project?

589. Specific - is the objective clear in terms of what, how, when, and where the situation will be changed?

590. Have external dependencies been captured in the schedule?

591. Is there an onboarding process in place?

592. Are staff skills known and available for each task?

593. Is stakeholder involvement adequate?

594. Did the ISO IEC 27002 project team have the right skills?

595. Is your organization certified as a supplier, wholesaler, regular dealer, or manufacturer of corresponding products/supplies?

596. Cost / benefit analysis?

597. Are people being developed to meet the challenges of the future?

598. Who needs training?

599. What were things that you did well, and could improve, and how?

600. Were stakeholders aware and supportive of the principles and practices of modern cost estimation?

601. Is the current culture aligned with the vision, mission, and values of the department?

602. What talent is needed?

603. Have activity relationships and interdependencies within tasks been adequately identified?

604. Are ISO IEC 27002 project contact logs kept up to date?

605. Is there a formal set of procedures supporting Issues Management?

606. Are there dependencies with other initiatives or ISO IEC 27002 projects?

2.30 Communications Management Plan: ISO IEC 27002

607. What to know?

608. Do you then often overlook a key stakeholder or stakeholder group?

609. Who is responsible?

610. How did the term stakeholder originate?

611. How will the person responsible for executing the communication item be notified?

612. How is this initiative related to other portfolios, programs, or ISO IEC 27002 projects?

613. Who are the members of the governing body?

614. Which stakeholders can influence others?

615. Are the stakeholders getting the information others need, are others consulted, are concerns addressed?

616. What approaches to you feel are the best ones to use?

617. What is the stakeholders level of authority?

618. What is the political influence?

619. What steps can you take for a positive relationship?

620. Why manage stakeholders?

621. Where do team members get information?

622. Are others part of the communications management plan?

623. Who is involved as you identify stakeholders?

624. Do you feel more overwhelmed by stakeholders?

625. Why do you manage communications?

2.31 Risk Management Plan: ISO IEC 27002

626. What is the probability the risk avoidance strategy will be successful?

627. Minimize cost and financial risk?

628. Market risk: will the new product be useful to your organization or marketable to others?

629. How quickly does this item need to be resolved?

630. What should be done with non-critical risks?

631. Is a software ISO IEC 27002 project management tool available?

632. What worked well?

633. Is the number of people on the ISO IEC 27002 project team adequate to do the job?

634. Are the reports useful and easy to read?

635. What are the chances the event will occur?

636. What things might go wrong?

637. How quickly does each item need to be resolved?

638. User involvement: do you have the right users?

639. How is the audit profession changing?

640. Who/what can assist?

641. Market risk -will the new service or product be useful to your organization or marketable to others?

642. Technology risk: is the ISO IEC 27002 project technically feasible?

643. Workarounds are determined during which step of risk management?

644. Can you stabilize dynamic risk factors?

645. What things are likely to change?

2.32 Risk Register: ISO IEC 27002

646. Schedule impact/severity estimated range (workdays) assume the event happens, what is the potential impact?

647. Do you require further engagement?

648. Methodology: how will risk management be performed on this ISO IEC 27002 project?

649. What will be done?

650. When would you develop a risk register?

651. What action, if any, has been taken to respond to the risk?

652. Cost/benefit – how much will the proposed mitigations cost and how does this cost compare with the potential cost of the risk event/situation should it occur?

653. How often will the Risk Management Plan and Risk Register be formally reviewed, and by whom?

654. What should you do when?

655. Are implemented controls working as others should?

656. What may happen or not go according to plan?

657. What further options might be available for

responding to the risk?

658. Budget and schedule: what are the estimated costs and schedules for performing risk-related activities?

659. Risk documentation: what reporting formats and processes will be used for risk management activities?

660. What is your current and future risk profile?

661. Who needs to know about this?

662. When is it going to be done?

663. Amongst the action plans and recommendations that you have to introduce are there some that could stop or delay the overall program?

664. What can be done about it?

665. People risk -are people with appropriate skills available to help complete the ISO IEC 27002 project?

2.33 Probability and Impact Assessment: ISO IEC 27002

666. What are the current demands of the customer?

667. What are the channels available for distribution to the customer?

668. Will new information become available during the ISO IEC 27002 project?

669. What should be the external organizations responsibility vis-à-vis total stake in the ISO IEC 27002 project?

670. Are enough people available?

671. What risks does your organization have if the ISO IEC 27002 projects fail to meet deadline?

672. Are ISO IEC 27002 project requirements stable?

673. Are testing tools available and suitable?

674. Who should be notified of the occurrence of each of the risk indicators?

675. What are the uncertainties associated with the technology selected for the ISO IEC 27002 project?

676. Assuming that you have identified a number of risks in the ISO IEC 27002 project, how would you prioritize them?

677. How completely has the customer been identified?

678. Which of your ISO IEC 27002 projects should be selected when compared with other ISO IEC 27002 projects?

679. What will be the impact or consequence if the risk occurs?

680. Which risks need to move on to Perform Quantitative Risk Analysis?

681. Are tools for analysis and design available?

682. How carefully have the potential competitors been identified?

683. How do the products attain the specifications?

2.34 Probability and Impact Matrix: ISO IEC 27002

684. How much risk do others need to take?

685. What are the preparations required for facing difficulties?

686. Can it be changed quickly?

687. How solid is the ISO IEC 27002 projection of competitive reaction?

688. Mandated delivery date?

689. What are the risks involved in appointing external agencies to manage the ISO IEC 27002 project?

690. Who has experience with this?

691. What is the risk appetite?

692. What are the uncertainties associated with the technology selected for the ISO IEC 27002 project?

693. Several experts are offsite, and wish to be included. How can this be done?

694. Do you have a mechanism for managing change?

695. Does the ISO IEC 27002 project team have experience with the technology to be implemented?

696. Are the risk data timely and relevant?

697. Does the customer have a solid idea of what is required?

698. Are compilers and code generators available and suitable for the product to be built?

699. Does the software engineering team have the right mix of skills?

700. What will be the likely political environment during the life of the ISO IEC 27002 project?

701. What should be done NEXT?

2.35 Risk Data Sheet: ISO IEC 27002

702. What is the likelihood of it happening?

703. What are the main opportunities available to you that you should grab while you can?

704. Has the most cost-effective solution been chosen?

705. Risk of what?

706. Has a sensitivity analysis been carried out?

707. Type of risk identified?

708. What can happen?

709. What do you know?

710. How can hazards be reduced?

711. What actions can be taken to eliminate or remove risk?

712. Do effective diagnostic tests exist?

713. What were the Causes that contributed?

714. What can you do?

715. What will be the consequences if it happens?

716. Will revised controls lead to tolerable risk levels?

717. How reliable is the data source?

718. What are you here for (Mission)?

719. What if client refuses?

720. How can it happen?

2.36 Procurement Management Plan: ISO IEC 27002

721. Has the budget been baselined?

722. Are all resource assumptions documented?

723. Are the ISO IEC 27002 project plans updated on a frequent basis?

724. Are action items captured and managed?

725. Are status reports received per the ISO IEC 27002 project Plan?

726. What are you trying to accomplish?

727. Have all team members been part of identifying risks?

728. ISO IEC 27002 project Objectives?

729. Do ISO IEC 27002 project managers participating in the ISO IEC 27002 project know the ISO IEC 27002 projects true status first hand?

730. Do ISO IEC 27002 project teams & team members report on status / activities / progress?

731. Was your organizations estimating methodology being used and followed?

732. Is there a Quality Management Plan?

733. How will the duration of the ISO IEC 27002 project influence your decisions?

2.37 Source Selection Criteria: ISO IEC 27002

734. What instructions should be provided regarding oral presentations?

735. How should comments received in response to a RFP be handled?

736. What past performance information should be requested?

737. What are the most common types of rating systems?

738. How are oral presentations documented?

739. What common questions or problems are associated with debriefings?

740. Have team members been adequately trained?

741. Do you consider all weaknesses, significant weaknesses, and deficiencies?

742. Is a letter of commitment from each proposed team member and key subcontractor included?

743. When should debriefings be held and how should they be scheduled?

744. What should a Draft Request for Proposal (DRFP) include?

745. What are the steps in performing a cost/tech tradeoff?

746. How is past performance evaluated?

747. Why promote competition?

748. What is the role of counsel in the procurement process?

749. What should clarifications include?

750. Have all evaluators been trained?

751. How should oral presentations be prepared for?

752. How do you manage procurement?

753. How organization are proposed quotes/prices?

2.38 Stakeholder Management Plan: ISO IEC 27002

754. How are stakeholders chosen and what roles might they have on a ISO IEC 27002 project?

755. Contradictory information between document sections?

756. What information should be collected?

757. Have the key elements of a coherent ISO IEC 27002 project management strategy been established?

758. How much information should be collected?

759. What inspection and testing is to be performed?

760. Are corrective actions and variances reported?

761. Are internal ISO IEC 27002 project status meetings held at reasonable intervals?

762. Have adequate resources been provided by management to ensure ISO IEC 27002 project success?

763. Have key stakeholders been identified?

764. Is the ISO IEC 27002 project sponsor clearly communicating the business case or rationale for why this ISO IEC 27002 project is needed?

765. What proven methodologies and standards will be used to ensure that materials, products, processes and services are fit for purpose?

766. Have all necessary approvals been obtained?

767. Are trade-offs between accepting the risk and mitigating the risk identified?

768. Are ISO IEC 27002 project team members involved in detailed estimating and scheduling?

769. Have ISO IEC 27002 project success criteria been defined?

2.39 Change Management Plan: ISO IEC 27002

770. Is it the same for each of the business units?

771. How can you best frame the message so that it addresses the audiences interests?

772. Has the training co-ordinator been provided with the training details and put in place the necessary arrangements?

773. What is the reason for the communication?

774. Which relationships will change?

775. Has a training need analysis been carried out?

776. Will a different work structure focus people on what is important?

777. What are the major changes to processes?

778. How do you know the requirements you documented are the right ones?

779. What risks may occur upfront?

780. What relationships will change?

781. Impact of systems implementation on organization change?

782. What are the specific target groups/audiences that will be impacted by this change?

783. Has the target training audience been identified and nominated?

784. Clearly articulate the overall business benefits of the ISO IEC 27002 project -why are you doing this now?

785. What new behaviours are required?

786. Why is the initiative is being undertaken - What are the business drivers?

787. Identify the current level of skills and knowledge and behaviours of the group that will be impacted on. What prerequisite knowledge do corresponding groups need?

788. What is the worst thing that can happen if you communicate information?

3.0 Executing Process Group: ISO IEC 27002

789. What is the shortest possible time it will take to complete this ISO IEC 27002 project?

790. How many different communication channels does the ISO IEC 27002 project team have?

791. Do schedule issues conflicts?

792. When is the appropriate time to bring the scorecard to Board meetings?

793. What is in place for ensuring adequate change control on ISO IEC 27002 projects that involve outside contracts?

794. On which process should team members spend the most time?

795. How do you enter durations, link tasks, and view critical path information?

796. Why do you need a good WBS to use ISO IEC 27002 project management software?

797. How well did the team follow the chosen processes?

798. Why is it important to determine activity sequencing on ISO IEC 27002 projects?

799. Will a new application be developed using existing hardware, software, and networks?

800. How can your organization use a weighted decision matrix to evaluate proposals as part of source selection?

801. Is the ISO IEC 27002 project making progress in helping to achieve the set results?

802. Who are the ISO IEC 27002 project stakeholders?

803. What type of information goes in the quality assurance plan?

804. Just how important is your work to the overall success of the ISO IEC 27002 project?

805. Is the ISO IEC 27002 project performing better or worse than planned?

806. It under budget or over budget?

3.1 Team Member Status Report: ISO IEC 27002

807. When a teams productivity and success depend on collaboration and the efficient flow of information, what generally fails them?

808. The problem with Reward & Recognition Programs is that the truly deserving people all too often get left out. How can you make it practical?

809. Is there evidence that staff is taking a more professional approach toward management of your organizations ISO IEC 27002 projects?

810. Why is it to be done?

811. How does this product, good, or service meet the needs of the ISO IEC 27002 project and your organization as a whole?

812. What specific interest groups do you have in place?

813. How can you make it practical?

814. How will resource planning be done?

815. Will the staff do training or is that done by a third party?

816. Does the product, good, or service already exist within your organization?

817. Does every department have to have a ISO IEC 27002 project Manager on staff?

818. Do you have an Enterprise ISO IEC 27002 project Management Office (EPMO)?

819. Are your organizations ISO IEC 27002 projects more successful over time?

820. How it is to be done?

821. Does your organization have the means (staff, money, contract, etc.) to produce or to acquire the product, good, or service?

822. Are the products of your organizations ISO IEC 27002 projects meeting customers objectives?

823. Are the attitudes of staff regarding ISO IEC 27002 project work improving?

824. What is to be done?

825. How much risk is involved?

3.2 Change Request: ISO IEC 27002

826. Who is communicating the change?

827. What are the requirements for urgent changes?

828. What are the duties of the change control team?

829. Why do you want to have a change control system?

830. Will all change requests and current status be logged?

831. Can you answer what happened, who did it, when did it happen, and what else will be affected?

832. Have all related configuration items been properly updated?

833. How does your organization control changes before and after software is released to a customer?

834. Describe how modifications, enhancements, defects and/or deficiencies shall be notified (e.g. Problem Reports, Change Requests etc) and managed. Detail warranty and/or maintenance periods?

835. Should a more thorough impact analysis be conducted?

836. How do team members communicate with each other?

837. Who is included in the change control team?

838. Where do changes come from?

839. Who needs to approve change requests?

840. How many lines of code must be changed to implement the change?

841. Will this change conflict with other requirements changes (e.g., lead to conflicting operational scenarios)?

842. Why were your requested changes rejected or not made?

843. Since there are no change requests in your ISO IEC 27002 project at this point, what must you have before you begin?

844. Which requirements attributes affect the risk to reliability the most?

845. Who will perform the change?

3.3 Change Log: ISO IEC 27002

846. How does this change affect the timeline of the schedule?

847. Who initiated the change request?

848. Is this a mandatory replacement?

849. Is the change request within ISO IEC 27002 project scope?

850. How does this change affect scope?

851. When was the request approved?

852. How does this relate to the standards developed for specific business processes?

853. Is the change request open, closed or pending?

854. Is the change backward compatible without limitations?

855. Is the requested change request a result of changes in other ISO IEC 27002 project(s)?

856. Do the described changes impact on the integrity or security of the system?

857. When was the request submitted?

858. Will the ISO IEC 27002 project fail if the change request is not executed?

859. Is the submitted change a new change or a modification of a previously approved change?

860. Does the suggested change request seem to represent a necessary enhancement to the product?

3.4 Decision Log: ISO IEC 27002

861. How consolidated and comprehensive a story can you tell by capturing currently available incident data in a central location and through a log of key decisions during an incident?

862. Which variables make a critical difference?

863. Does anything need to be adjusted?

864. How does the use a Decision Support System influence the strategies/tactics or costs?

865. How do you define success?

866. Decision-making process; how will the team make decisions?

867. It becomes critical to track and periodically revisit both operational effectiveness; Are you noticing all that you need to, and are you interpreting what you see effectively?

868. What makes you different or better than others companies selling the same thing?

869. What was the rationale for the decision?

870. What alternatives/risks were considered?

871. How does an increasing emphasis on cost containment influence the strategies and tactics used?

872. With whom was the decision shared or considered?

873. What eDiscovery problem or issue did your organization set out to fix or make better?

874. What are the cost implications?

875. What is the line where eDiscovery ends and document review begins?

876. Is your opponent open to a non-traditional workflow, or will it likely challenge anything you do?

877. Behaviors; what are guidelines that the team has identified that will assist them with getting the most out of team meetings?

878. What is your overall strategy for quality control / quality assurance procedures?

879. Adversarial environment. is your opponent open to a non-traditional workflow, or will it likely challenge anything you do?

880. Do strategies and tactics aimed at less than full control reduce the costs of management or simply shift the cost burden?

3.5 Quality Audit: ISO IEC 27002

881. How does your organization know that its systems for meeting staff extracurricular learning support requirements are appropriately effective and constructive?

882. How does your organization know that its relationships with industry and employers are appropriately effective and constructive?

883. Does the supplier use a formal quality system?

884. Are training programs documented?

885. How does your organization know that its staff financial services are appropriately effective and constructive?

886. How does your organization know that its research planning and management systems are appropriately effective and constructive in enabling quality research outcomes?

887. How does your organization know that the research supervision provided to its staff is appropriately effective and constructive?

888. How does the organization know that its system for maintaining and advancing the capabilities of its staff, particularly in relation to the Mission of the organization, is appropriately effective and constructive?

889. Are adequate and conveniently located toilet facilities available for use by the employees?

890. How does your organization know that its systems for providing high quality consultancy services to external parties are appropriately effective and constructive?

891. Can your organization demonstrate exactly how and why results were achieved?

892. Is quality audit a prerequisite for program accreditation or program recognition?

893. How does your organization know that its public relations and marketing systems are appropriately effective and constructive?

894. How does your organization know that its systems for communicating with and among staff are appropriately effective and constructive?

895. How does your organization know that its financial management system is appropriately effective and constructive?

896. How does your organization know that its systems for assisting staff with career planning and employment placements are appropriately effective and constructive?

897. Are there appropriate means for intervening if necessary?

898. How does your organization ensure that equipment is appropriately maintained and

producing valid results?

899. Does the report read coherently?

900. How does your organization know that its research programs are appropriately effective and constructive?

3.6 Team Directory: ISO IEC 27002

901. Where should the information be distributed?

902. Process decisions: are all start-up, turn over and close out requirements of the contract satisfied?

903. Who will talk to the customer?

904. Process decisions: are contractors adequately prosecuting the work?

905. Do purchase specifications and configurations match requirements?

906. Who will write the meeting minutes and distribute?

907. Process decisions: do invoice amounts match accepted work in place?

908. Who will report ISO IEC 27002 project status to all stakeholders?

909. When will you produce deliverables?

910. Process decisions: which organizational elements and which individuals will be assigned management functions?

911. How does the team resolve conflicts and ensure tasks are completed?

912. Who should receive information (all

stakeholders)?

913. Who are the Team Members?

914. Process decisions: do job conditions warrant additional actions to collect job information and document on-site activity?

915. Why is the work necessary?

916. Decisions: what could be done better to improve the quality of the constructed product?

917. How will the team handle changes?

918. Have you decided when to celebrate the ISO IEC 27002 projects completion date?

919. Days from the time the issue is identified?

3.7 Team Operating Agreement: ISO IEC 27002

920. How does teaming fit in with overall organizational goals and meet organizational needs?

921. Did you draft the meeting agenda?

922. What is culture?

923. Did you prepare participants for the next meeting?

924. Seconds for members to respond?

925. Has the appropriate access to relevant data and analysis capability been granted?

926. Are there more than two native languages represented by your team?

927. What are some potential sources of conflict among team members?

928. How will your group handle planned absences?

929. Do you brief absent members after they view meeting notes or listen to a recording?

930. Communication protocols: how will the team communicate?

931. Do you call or email participants to ensure

understanding, follow-through and commitment to the meeting outcomes?

932. Do team members reside in more than two countries?

933. Does your team need access to all documents and information at all times?

934. Are there more than two national cultures represented by your team?

935. Is compensation based on team and individual performance?

936. Confidentiality: how will confidential information be handled?

937. What are the boundaries (organizational or geographic) within which you operate?

938. How will you divide work equitably?

939. Do you leverage technology engagement tools group chat, polls, screen sharing, etc.?

3.8 Team Performance Assessment: ISO IEC 27002

940. Is there a particular method of data analysis that you would recommend as a means of demonstrating that method variance is not of great concern for a given dataset?

941. How do you recognize and praise members for contributions?

942. To what degree are sub-teams possible or necessary?

943. Where to from here?

944. Which situations call for a more extreme type of adaptiveness in which team members actually re-define roles?

945. Can team performance be reliably measured in simulator and live exercises using the same assessment tool?

946. To what degree does the teams work approach provide opportunity for members to engage in open interaction?

947. To what degree can team members meet frequently enough to accomplish the teams ends?

948. To what degree do team members understand one anothers roles and skills?

949. To what degree are the skill areas critical to team performance present?

950. Do friends perform better than acquaintances?

951. To what degree are the teams goals and objectives clear, simple, and measurable?

952. If you have received criticism from reviewers that your work suffered from method variance, what was the circumstance?

953. To what degree are fresh input and perspectives systematically caught and added (for example, through information and analysis, new members, and senior sponsors)?

954. To what degree is there a sense that only the team can succeed?

955. To what degree will new and supplemental skills be introduced as the need is recognized?

956. Social categorization and intergroup behaviour: Does minimal intergroup discrimination make social identity more positive?

957. If you are worried about method variance before you collect data, what sort of design elements might you include to reduce or eliminate the threat of method variance?

958. To what degree can the team ensure that all members are individually and jointly accountable for the teams purpose, goals, approach, and work-

products?

959. Can familiarity breed backup?

3.9 Team Member Performance Assessment: ISO IEC 27002

960. What stakeholders must be involved in the development and oversight of the performance plan?

961. In what areas would you like to concentrate your knowledge and resources?

962. What types of learning are targeted (e.g., cognitive, affective, psychomotor, procedural)?

963. How are assessments designed, delivered, and otherwise used to maximize training?

964. What are acceptable governance changes?

965. To what degree do team members articulate the teams work approach?

966. What qualities does a successful Team leader possess?

967. Is there reluctance to join a team?

968. What steps have you taken to improve performance?

969. What is the role of the Reviewer?

970. What resources do you need?

971. What is collaboration?

972. What is the Business Management Oversight Process?

973. How are performance measures and associated incentives developed?

974. What evaluation results did you have?

975. What evaluation results do you have?

976. What tools are available to determine whether all contract functional and compliance areas of performance objectives, measures, and incentives have been met?

977. To what degree does the teams purpose contain themes that are particularly meaningful and memorable?

978. For what period of time is a member rated?

979. To what degree are the relative importance and priority of the goals clear to all team members?

3.10 Issue Log: ISO IEC 27002

980. How do you manage communications?

981. Are there too many who have an interest in some aspect of your work?

982. Which team member will work with each stakeholder?

983. Are stakeholder roles recognized by your organization?

984. What is the status of the issue?

985. Why not more evaluators?

986. In classifying stakeholders, which approach to do so are you using?

987. Can an impact cause deviation beyond team, stage or ISO IEC 27002 project tolerances?

988. Is the issue log kept in a safe place?

989. What is the stakeholders political influence?

990. Is access to the Issue Log controlled?

991. Persistence; will users learn a work around or will they be bothered every time?

992. Who have you worked with in past, similar initiatives?

993. Do you feel a register helps?

994. What does the stakeholder need from the team?

995. Are the stakeholders getting the information they need, are they consulted, are concerns addressed?

4.0 Monitoring and Controlling Process Group: ISO IEC 27002

996. Does the solution fit in with organizations technical architectural requirements?

997. User: who wants the information and what are they interested in?

998. When will the ISO IEC 27002 project be done?

999. What departments are involved in its daily operation?

1000. Key stakeholders to work with. How many potential communications channels exist on the ISO IEC 27002 project?

1001. How to ensure validity, quality and consistency?

1002. Change, where should you look for problems?

1003. How well did you do?

1004. Did the ISO IEC 27002 project team have the right skills?

1005. What are the goals of the program?

1006. Is there sufficient time allotted between the general system design and the detailed system design phases?

1007. Where is the Risk in the ISO IEC 27002 project?

1008. What areas does the group agree are the biggest success on the ISO IEC 27002 project?

1009. What is the timeline for the ISO IEC 27002 project?

1010. Is there adequate validation on required fields?

1011. Based on your ISO IEC 27002 project communication management plan, what worked well?

1012. Just how important is your work to the overall success of the ISO IEC 27002 project?

4.1 Project Performance Report: ISO IEC 27002

1013. To what degree does the teams approach to its work allow for modification and improvement over time?

1014. To what degree are the goals realistic?

1015. To what degree does the information network provide individuals with the information they require?

1016. To what degree will the team ensure that all members equitably share the work essential to the success of the team?

1017. To what degree are the goals ambitious?

1018. To what degree can team members vigorously define the teams purpose in considerations with others who are not part of the functioning team?

1019. How will procurement be coordinated with other ISO IEC 27002 project aspects, such as scheduling and performance reporting?

1020. To what degree are the demands of the task compatible with and converge with the relationships of the informal organization?

1021. To what degree will the team adopt a concrete, clearly understood, and agreed-upon approach that will result in achievement of the teams goals?

1022. To what degree does the teams purpose constitute a broader, deeper aspiration than just accomplishing short-term goals?

1023. To what degree are the tasks requirements reflected in the flow and storage of information?

1024. To what degree is the information network consistent with the structure of the formal organization?

1025. To what degree can the team measure progress against specific goals?

1026. What is the degree to which rules govern information exchange between groups?

1027. To what degree does the formal organization make use of individual resources and meet individual needs?

1028. To what degree do team members agree with the goals, relative importance, and the ways in which achievement will be measured?

4.2 Variance Analysis: ISO IEC 27002

1029. Can the relationship with problem customers be restructured so that there is a win-win situation?

1030. How are material, labor, and overhead standards set?

1031. Are all cwbs elements specified for external reporting?

1032. Does the contractor use objective results, design reviews and tests to trace schedule performance?

1033. Is budgeted cost for work performed calculated in a manner consistent with the way work is planned?

1034. Are control accounts opened and closed based on the start and completion of work contained therein?

1035. What is the incurrence of actual indirect costs in excess of budgets, by element of expense?

1036. Is cost and schedule performance measurement done in a consistent, systematic manner?

1037. What is the dollar amount of the fluctuation?

1038. What does an unfavorable overhead volume variance mean?

1039. Contemplated overhead expenditure for each

period based on the best information currently is available?

1040. How does the use of a single conversion element (rather than the traditional labor and overhead elements) affect standard costing?

1041. Are indirect costs charged to the appropriate indirect pools and incurring organization?

1042. What is the budgeted cost for work scheduled?

1043. Are data elements reconcilable between internal summary reports and reports forwarded to the stakeholders?

1044. Are procedures for variance analysis documented and consistently applied at the control account level and selected WBS and organizational levels at least monthly as a routine task?

1045. Does the contractors system provide unit or lot costs when applicable?

1046. Why do variances exist?

1047. Is the entire contract planned in time-phased control accounts to the extent practicable?

4.3 Earned Value Status: ISO IEC 27002

1048. Where are your problem areas?

1049. Are you hitting your ISO IEC 27002 projects targets?

1050. How does this compare with other ISO IEC 27002 projects?

1051. Validation is a process of ensuring that the developed system will actually achieve the stakeholders desired outcomes; Are you building the right product? What do you validate?

1052. If earned value management (EVM) is so good in determining the true status of a ISO IEC 27002 project and ISO IEC 27002 project its completion, why is it that hardly any one uses it in information systems related ISO IEC 27002 projects?

1053. Verification is a process of ensuring that the developed system satisfies the stakeholders agreements and specifications; Are you building the product right? What do you verify?

1054. What is the unit of forecast value?

1055. Earned value can be used in almost any ISO IEC 27002 project situation and in almost any ISO IEC 27002 project environment. it may be used on large ISO IEC 27002 projects, medium sized ISO IEC 27002 projects, tiny ISO IEC 27002 projects (in cut-down form), complex and simple ISO IEC 27002 projects and in any market sector. some people, of course, know all about earned value, they have used it for years - but perhaps not as effectively as they could have?

1056. How much is it going to cost by the finish?

1057. Where is evidence-based earned value in your organization reported?

1058. When is it going to finish?

4.4 Risk Audit: ISO IEC 27002

1059. Who audits the auditor?

1060. How do you manage risk?

1061. Are end-users enthusiastically committed to the ISO IEC 27002 project and the system/product to be built?

1062. What is the anticipated volatility of the requirements?

1063. Are staff committed for the duration of the product?

1064. Do you have a realistic budget and do you present regular financial reports that identify how you are going against that budget?

1065. Are you meeting your legal, regulatory and compliance requirements - if not, why not?

1066. Is your organization willing to commit significant time to the requirements gathering process?

1067. The halo effect in business risk audits: can strategic risk assessment bias auditor judgment about accounting details?

1068. Can assurance be expanded beyond the traditional audit without undermining independence?

1069. For paid staff, does your organization comply with the minimum conditions for employment and/or the applicable modern award?

1070. Is the customer technically sophisticated in the product area?

1071. Does your organization have any policies or procedures to guide its decision-making (code of conduct for the board, conflict of interest policy, etc.)?

1072. Are contracts reviewed before renewal?

1073. Do you have a consistent repeatable process that is actually used?

1074. How effective are your risk controls?

1075. Does your organization have or has considered the need for insurance covers: public liability, professional indemnity and directors and officers liability?

4.5 Contractor Status Report: ISO IEC 27002

1076. Are there contractual transfer concerns?

1077. What was the budget or estimated cost for your organizations services?

1078. If applicable; describe your standard schedule for new software version releases. Are new software version releases included in the standard maintenance plan?

1079. What is the average response time for answering a support call?

1080. Describe how often regular updates are made to the proposed solution. Are corresponding regular updates included in the standard maintenance plan?

1081. How does the proposed individual meet each requirement?

1082. What process manages the contracts?

1083. How is risk transferred?

1084. What was the final actual cost?

1085. Who can list a ISO IEC 27002 project as organization experience, your organization or a previous employee of your organization?

1086. How long have you been using the services?

1087. What are the minimum and optimal bandwidth requirements for the proposed solution?

1088. What was the actual budget or estimated cost for your organizations services?

1089. What was the overall budget or estimated cost?

4.6 Formal Acceptance: ISO IEC 27002

1090. Does it do what ISO IEC 27002 project team said it would?

1091. General estimate of the costs and times to complete the ISO IEC 27002 project?

1092. What lessons were learned about your ISO IEC 27002 project management methodology?

1093. Did the ISO IEC 27002 project manager and team act in a professional and ethical manner?

1094. Did the ISO IEC 27002 project achieve its MOV?

1095. Do you buy-in installation services?

1096. How does your team plan to obtain formal acceptance on your ISO IEC 27002 project?

1097. How well did the team follow the methodology?

1098. What function(s) does it fill or meet?

1099. Was the client satisfied with the ISO IEC 27002 project results?

1100. What was done right?

1101. Was the ISO IEC 27002 project goal achieved?

1102. What can you do better next time?

1103. What are the requirements against which to test, Who will execute?

1104. Was the sponsor/customer satisfied?

1105. Was the ISO IEC 27002 project managed well?

1106. Who would use it?

1107. Is formal acceptance of the ISO IEC 27002 project product documented and distributed?

1108. What is the Acceptance Management Process?

1109. Do you perform formal acceptance or burn-in tests?

5.0 Closing Process Group: ISO IEC 27002

1110. How well defined and documented were the ISO IEC 27002 project management processes you chose to use?

1111. If a risk event occurs, what will you do?

1112. What is the risk of failure to your organization?

1113. Are there funding or time constraints?

1114. Will the ISO IEC 27002 project deliverable(s) replace a current asset or group of assets?

1115. What were things that you need to improve?

1116. How well did the chosen processes fit the needs of the ISO IEC 27002 project?

1117. What can you do better next time, and what specific actions can you take to improve?

1118. Did the delivered product meet the specified requirements and goals of the ISO IEC 27002 project?

1119. Can the lesson learned be replicated?

1120. Did you do things well?

1121. Did the ISO IEC 27002 project management methodology work?

1122. Is the ISO IEC 27002 project funded?

1123. Contingency planning. if a risk event occurs, what will you do?

1124. What level of risk does the proposed budget represent to the ISO IEC 27002 project?

1125. Is this a follow-on to a previous ISO IEC 27002 project?

5.1 Procurement Audit: ISO IEC 27002

1126. Was your organization specific about the nature and scope of the performance before launching the procurement process?

1127. Has an upper limit of cost been fixed?

1128. Are information gathered to produce knowledge about procured goods and services, prices paid and supplier performance?

1129. Does your organization have an overall procurement strategy and/or policy?

1130. Is there an effective risk management system continuously monitoring procurement risk?

1131. Are proper authorization and approval required prior to payment?

1132. Are internal control mechanisms performed before payments?

1133. Does your organization make sources of information beyond the tender documents equally available for all the candidates?

1134. When corresponding references were made, was a precise description of the performance not otherwise possible and were the already stated references accompanied by the words or equivalent?

1135. Is there a practice that prohibits signing blank

purchase orders?

1136. Did you consider and evaluate alternatives, like bundling needs with other departments or grouping supplies in separate lots with different characteristics?

1137. Are criteria and sub-criteria set suitable to identify the tender that offers best value for money?

1138. Is funding made available for payments under the contract at the appropriate time and in accordance with the relevant national/public financial procedures?

1139. Does the strategy ensure that needs are met, and not exceeded?

1140. Are employees with cash disbursement responsibilities required to take scheduled vacations?

1141. Are there procedures governing the negotiations of long-term contracts?

1142. Which are the main risks and controls of each phase?

1143. Is there a system in place to handle partial delivery of orders, back orders, and partial payments?

1144. Is the opportunity properly published?

1145. Do the internal control systems function appropriate?

5.2 Contract Close-Out: ISO IEC 27002

1146. Was the contract type appropriate?

1147. Why Outsource?

1148. Change in knowledge?

1149. Parties: who is involved?

1150. Have all acceptance criteria been met prior to final payment to contractors?

1151. Was the contract complete without requiring numerous changes and revisions?

1152. What is capture management?

1153. Was the contract sufficiently clear so as not to result in numerous disputes and misunderstandings?

1154. What happens to the recipient of services?

1155. How is the contracting office notified of the automatic contract close-out?

1156. Has each contract been audited to verify acceptance and delivery?

1157. How does it work?

1158. Have all contract records been included in the ISO IEC 27002 project archives?

1159. Change in attitude or behavior?

1160. Parties: Authorized?

1161. How/when used ?

1162. Are the signers the authorized officials?

1163. Change in circumstances?

1164. Have all contracts been completed?

1165. Have all contracts been closed?

5.3 Project or Phase Close-Out: ISO IEC 27002

1166. What is a Risk?

1167. What security considerations needed to be addressed during the procurement life cycle?

1168. Who exerted influence that has positively affected or negatively impacted the ISO IEC 27002 project?

1169. What was learned?

1170. What hierarchical authority does the stakeholder have in your organization?

1171. In preparing the Lessons Learned report, should it reflect a consensus viewpoint, or should the report reflect the different individual viewpoints?

1172. What was expected from each stakeholder?

1173. What process was planned for managing issues/ risks?

1174. How often did each stakeholder need an update?

1175. What benefits or impacts does the stakeholder group expect to obtain as a result of the ISO IEC 27002 project?

1176. What were the desired outcomes?

1177. Planned completion date?

1178. Were risks identified and mitigated?

1179. Who controlled the resources for the ISO IEC 27002 project?

1180. What are the mandatory communication needs for each stakeholder?

1181. How much influence did the stakeholder have over others?

1182. What are they?

1183. What are the informational communication needs for each stakeholder?

5.4 Lessons Learned: ISO IEC 27002

1184. Were all interests adequately involved/ informed?

1185. Which estimation issues did you personally have and what was the impact?

1186. How well was ISO IEC 27002 project status communicated throughout your involvement in the ISO IEC 27002 project?

1187. How efficient and effective were meetings?

1188. Would you spend your own money to fix this issue?

1189. How much communication is socially oriented?

1190. What did you put in place to ensure success?

1191. Are you in full regulatory compliance?

1192. What mistakes did you successfully avoid making?

1193. How was the quality of products/processes assured?

1194. Is there any way in which you think your development process hampered this ISO IEC 27002 project?

1195. Why does your organization need a lessons

learned (LL) capability?

1196. What solutions or recommendations can you offer that would have improved some aspect of the ISO IEC 27002 project?

1197. Were cost budgets met?

1198. Who had fiscal authority to manage the funding for the ISO IEC 27002 project, did that work?

1199. What is in the future?

1200. What would you approach differently next time?

1201. Whom to share Lessons Learned Information with?

1202. What was the single greatest success and the single greatest shortcoming or challenge from the ISO IEC 27002 projects perspective?

1203. How well defined were the acceptance criteria for ISO IEC 27002 project deliverables?

Index

clarifies 16
clarify   20-21, 25-26, 29-35, 39, 55, 59, 61, 65, 69, 73, 97, 99-100, 102-103, 107-109, 111, 113, 115-116, 118-119, 121
classified   124
clearly 10, 15, 18, 24, 39, 41, 54, 67, 79, 95, 144, 154, 190, 210, 213, 240
client   137, 205, 250
closed 92, 156, 220, 242, 257
closely 9
Close-Out   6, 256, 258
Closing 6, 57, 252
Coaches   25
coding 150
cognitive   234
coherent   139, 210
coherently   226
collect 54, 178, 228, 232
collected   31, 37, 41, 45, 63, 73, 210
collection   49-52, 58
coming   65
comments   208
commercial   154
commit   246
commitment   124, 186, 208, 230
committed   61, 139, 183, 192, 246
Committee   149, 175
common   130, 208
community   170, 178
companies   1, 120, 222
company   7
compare   198, 244
compared   180, 201
comparison   10, 153
compatible   220, 240
compelling   33
competence   51
competent   104
compilers   203
complete   1, 8, 10, 37, 45, 156-157, 168, 171, 185, 190, 199, 214, 250, 256
completed   11, 26, 29, 34, 36, 109, 157, 163, 169, 227, 257
completely   170, 201
completing   151

imbedded   79
immediate   43
impact 4, 25, 43, 45, 47-48, 50, 76, 169, 174, 198, 200-202, 212,
218, 220, 236, 260
impacted   128, 213, 258
impacts   42, 258
implement   34, 56, 64, 79, 88, 112, 119, 219
importance   235, 241
important   19, 22, 55-56, 98, 101, 103, 112, 118, 135, 142,
166, 183, 212, 214-215, 239
improve   2, 9, 67, 69-71, 73-77, 131, 169, 193, 228, 234, 252
improved   67, 70, 74-75, 85, 261
improves   128
improving   77, 217
inactions   22
incentives   88, 235
incident   31, 62, 97, 102, 120, 222
incidents   18, 44, 63, 86, 89, 93-94, 96, 106, 110, 118, 120
include   19, 74, 77, 154, 156-157, 208-209, 232
included   2, 7, 51, 111, 135, 143, 149, 170, 176, 178, 202,
208, 219, 248, 256
includes   9, 49
including   25-26, 38, 42, 73, 87, 130, 150, 188
increase   72, 149
increasing   222
incurred   46
incurrence   189, 242
incurring   243
indemnity   247
in-depth   8, 10
indicate   47, 80
indicated   83
indicators   21, 46, 60, 87, 154, 200
indirect   153-154, 176, 188-189, 242-243
indirectly   1
individual   1, 124, 171, 230, 241, 248, 258
industry   101, 106, 224
influence   132, 135, 194, 207, 222, 236, 258-259
inform 34
informal   240
informed   260
inherent   191
inhibit 72

monitor   76, 80-84, 86, 88-89, 92-93, 178
monitored   84, 86, 128, 169
monitoring   5, 80-81, 84-86, 89-90, 94, 165, 189, 238, 254
monthly   243
motivate   101, 111
motivation   18, 88, 131
motive 186
moving   112
narrow 62
national   90-91, 230, 255
native 229
nature 45, 119, 154, 254
nearest   11
necessary   55, 57, 63, 72, 136, 153, 178, 189, 211-212, 221,
225, 228, 231
needed   20-21, 37, 58, 86, 176, 179, 186, 193, 210, 258
negatively   258
neither 1
network   3, 163-164, 240-241
networks   85, 215
Neutral 10, 15, 24, 41, 54, 67, 79, 95
nominated   213
normal 154
notice 1, 168
noticing   222
notified   194, 200, 218, 256
notify   17, 19, 97, 110
number   22, 40, 53, 65, 78, 94, 125, 166, 196, 200, 262
numerous   256
objective   7, 130, 154, 180, 192, 242
objectives   16, 19-20, 24, 30, 59, 108, 156, 168, 206, 217, 232,
235
observed   75
observing   182
obstacles   19, 179
obtain 250, 258
obtained   31, 211
obviously   10
occurred   102
occurrence   200
occurring   77, 128
occurs 51, 60, 201, 252-253
offence   95

replace   131, 252
replaced   136
replicated   252
report 5-6, 80, 91, 93, 99, 113, 206, 216, 226-227, 240, 248, 258
reported   153, 210, 245
reporting   62, 86, 104, 117, 120, 185, 199, 240, 242
reports 43, 103, 115, 122, 132, 137, 155, 176, 196, 206, 218, 243, 246
represent   180, 221, 253
reproduced   1
request   5, 141, 180, 208, 218, 220-221
requested   1, 74, 208, 219-220
requests   218-219
require 27-28, 38, 52, 91, 130, 165, 198, 240
required   18, 21, 24-26, 29, 33-34, 37-38, 44, 55, 71, 133, 136, 143, 157, 159, 171, 184, 190, 202-203, 213, 239, 254-255
requires   58
requiring   132, 256
research   96, 161, 224, 226
reserved   1
reserves   156
reside 177, 230
resilience   16, 20, 110, 115
resolution   57, 62
resolve 18-19, 227
resolved   20, 89, 176, 192, 196
resource   3-4, 140, 142, 150, 165-167, 192, 206, 216
resources   2, 7, 29, 33, 37, 73, 81, 85-86, 108, 121, 139, 147, 149, 155, 157, 159, 164, 170, 178, 180, 210, 234, 241, 259
respect   1, 43, 120
respective   135
respond   86, 198, 229
responded   11
responding   199
response   58, 79-80, 83, 92, 97, 208, 248
responsive   170, 178
restrict 82
result   57, 178, 181, 184, 220, 240, 256, 258
resulted   79
resulting   54, 137, 147
results 8, 28, 35, 49, 67, 72-73, 87, 89, 128, 135-137, 159, 176, 178, 215, 225-226, 235, 242, 250
retain 88, 93, 95

Lightning Source UK Ltd.
Milton Keynes UK
UKHW010909210919
350180UK00011B/577/P